In appreciation of your friendship
& the many hours of service to
our Lord.

Christmas 1974

B.P. Business Nelson

The Way
of the
Master

THE WAY OF THE MASTER

MARK E. PETERSEN

BOOKCRAFT INC.
SALT LAKE CITY, UTAH

COPYRIGHT © 1974 BY
BOOKCRAFT, INC.

Library of Congress Catalog Card Number: 74-19505

ISBN 0-88494-271-6

2nd Printing, 1974

LITHOGRAPHED IN U.S.A.

PUBLISHERS PRESS
SALT LAKE CITY, UTAH

"He that soweth to his flesh shall of the flesh reap corruption; but he that soweth to the Spirit shall of the Spirit reap life everlasting."

(GALATIANS 6:8.)

Contents

Preface

THIS BOOK IS DEDICATED

to righteous living and truthful teaching of gospel principles.

When the Savior said that the gate is strait and the way is narrow "which leadeth unto life, and few there be that find it" (Matt. 7:14), he taught almost in the same breath: "Beware of false prophets, which come to you in sheep's clothing, but inwardly they are ravening wolves." (Verse 15.)

He added still another caution: "Not every one that saith unto me, Lord, Lord, shall enter into the kingdom of heaven; but he that doeth the will of my Father which is in heaven." (Verse 21.)

How plaintive was Eve's confession after partaking of the forbidden fruit: "The serpent beguiled me, and I did eat." (Gen. 3:13.)

It is so with all of us when we yield to transgression, to persuasions of false teachers, or when we tend to become atheistic. We are beguiled as was Eve by that selfsame serpent, Lucifer, the fallen angel.

This volume contains many of the warnings given by the prophets of God to protect us from error. The armor of the Holy Spirit will shield us if only we will listen to those warnings.

Chapter 1

The Longest War

It has been a long conflict — this war that Satan fights.

He is an unyielding enemy, an untiring and relentless foe. He has neither mercy nor pity. Compassion is farthest from his mind. He delights in cruelty and takes sadistic pleasure in bringing misery to human beings.

Satan hates humans, because he was not allowed to become human himself. Jealousy, envy, deep resentment — call it what you will, but he is full of it.

And frustration? He is plagued by it every moment. That is one thing that makes him as he is. He was frustrated in his evil effort in our preexistent life as he sought by guile, intrigue and force to seize the throne of the Almighty.

He coveted honor, prestige and glory; he wanted the adulation and praise of others; he sought to be lifted up above the rest. What an egotist!

Lucifer hated his elder brother, Jehovah, and when Jehovah's plan was accepted over his own, Lucifer's rage knew no bounds. Blinded by jealousy, enraged by his own defeat, he sought to thwart everything that Jehovah stood for, everything Jehovah did.

So he declared war on the Savior. It was a war in heaven. When we think of heaven as a place of sublime tranquility, a haven of peace and rest, and then think of such a conflict in the midst of it, we can begin to understand the bitterness of Lucifer.

He brought the spirit of hell into the presence of God and made the celestial world a battleground.

But Michael, the mighty archangel of God, who always has defended Jehovah and stands by his side, rallied the faithful and cast Lucifer out of heaven, together with all who followed him, for there were others who were likewise crazed by lust for power, converted by the persuasive influence of Lucifer.

These unfortunates numbered a third of the hosts of heaven. They were caught in the same vicious circle as was their leader: ambition, frustration, and then rebellion.

Cast out of heaven, Lucifer and his devilish host turned to the next step in their nefarious warfare — enticement!

They had wanted to become mortals and have physical bodies like ours, but were defeated by their own rebellion. However, they knew that mortals would be subject to sin and would have weaknesses, and that many of them would surrender to enticement.

So Lucifer's army turned to temptation as their most effective weapon. They would induce these mortals to sin and by this means endeavor to defeat the purposes of Jehovah, who by peaceful and righteous means, would help each mortal toward perfection.

Lucifer had sought to become like God — that was his great ambition — but he chose the wrong way of doing so.

Now he sought to prevent all of us from becoming like our Father in heaven as we use the right means, the way provided by Jehovah. Seeing that the gospel plan truly can make mortals perfect like God only added to the frustration of Lucifer.

He sees us advance toward divinity by Christ's plan. He knows that he never can achieve it, worlds without end, and so his frustration is multiplied. His determination to prevent our progress becomes even more intense; therefore he continues his war against us here on earth, and his prime targets are the Saints.

He knows what exaltation means, for he saw it as he lived in the presence of God, where he himself once held high authority. (D&C 76:25.)

He knows that "all that my Father hath" shall be given to His faithful children (D&C 84:38), and he knows that such is now forever beyond his reach. So once again in him there arises deeper frustration, sharper resentment, and more vicious anger.

Jealousy against the Savior and all of his Saints increases in his evil heart. He uses every tool of enticement and temptation to accomplish his wicked ends. Inasmuch as he himself now can never be exalted, he tries to prevent all others from achieving that goal.

What does he care about us, except to destroy us? We are his targets, we are his prey. With lies and intrigue he would persuade us that happiness may be found in sin, that gain may be had through fraud, deception, licentiousness, and even murder.

By his glamor he would blind us to the end result of sin. He would make it seem attractive, even though he knows that its wage is death.

He lures us by the lust of the flesh. He resents "the flesh" because he knows that he himself can never have it.

He takes advantage of our free agency and our human tendencies in his fight to destroy us. He knows that the Lord gave us weaknesses to make us humble, so he uses these very weaknesses to bring about our destruction.

He therefore tempts us according to the flesh with sex, money, greed, worldly prestige, ease, comfort, and a loose and carefree life.

With it he introduces philosophies to counteract the teachings of Christ. And so we have atheism to feed the conceit of so-called intellectualism, and counterfeit religions for those who wish to believe in God. To blind the pious he brings forth false gods, false prophets, false creeds and churches which have a form of godliness but deny the power thereof.

With every conceivable device he wages war with the Saints, endeavoring to make them miserable like himself, always seeking to thwart the purposes of Jehovah against whom his jealousy and resentment know no end.

Chapter 2

Desire

There is a devil, as surely as there is a God. His deceiving influence is all about us, even as is the ennobling Spirit of heaven.

Both good and evil beckon us, and yet there are some who pretend to ignore them both. They blissfully say with the poet: "I am the master of my fate."

But are they? Could what they call self-mastery slip into other hands and make them slaves?

For the most part we do forge our own lives. It is true that generally we chart our own course. Our ultimate destiny, after all is said, is nevertheless within our own two hands.

But we must recognize that we walk a path with good on one side and evil on the other. Each beckons and entreats us. What we do will depend on what we really want from life. To which enticement will our inner self respond? What is it we really and truly seek?

An opinion poll among college students asked those questions and brought forth one united response: "Happiness." And that is the basic hope of every human being.

But the way to achieve it is a perplexing question to most, and definitions of happiness certainly vary. What is happiness, and where shall we find it? Will we obtain what we want in goodness, or in contrary paths?

Some may narrow it down to daily comfort and the fulfilling of our physical needs. Some know that happiness is only to be found in ennobling the soul.

But others prefer compromising situations wherein they can be pious a little and sin a little, and hope to find enjoyment in both. They tell themselves that it is good to be broad-minded and that this is the way it is done.

The desire of our heart, whether it be the craving of the flesh or a thirst for righteousness, will determine the way we go.

Desire! Desire! If it is for the flesh, meaning any form of worldliness, we should recognize its source. Our sense of values must be weighed constantly, and checked and rechecked.

Is money our goal? Is self-gratification, or prestige, or adulation, or popularity with the crowd? Do we have a mania for sex or liquor or narcotics? Is it covetousness? Is it an inordinate desire for food?

Or could it be a desire to bask in the questionable light of so-called intellectualism and indulge in human philosophies — be they ever so scholarly — which nevertheless are based on the uninspired deductions of men?

These are all of the flesh, all of the earth, earthy.

Let us remember that desire, like all other human passions, can be controlled and properly directed. Evil enticements may be recognized and avoided.

As every well-balanced person knows, our desire truly should be a hunger and a thirst after righteousness, an earnest reach for God, because we are promised that we can become like him.

If we but understood this inspiring fact, there could be no room whatever in our minds for objectives of the flesh.

Our basic desires form the measure of our characters. If we love the light we shall seek it and learn to become like God. But if our desires are evil we shall prefer darkness over light and shall find it.

It was the apostle Paul who said: "They that are after the flesh do mind the things of the flesh; but they that are after the Spirit the things of the Spirit. For to be carnally minded is death; but to be spiritually minded is life and peace." (Rom. 8:5, 6.)

Are not life and peace what we all really seek?

But our difficulty is making up our minds as to the manner of seeking. Experience demonstrates that wickedness never was happiness. Joy comes only in righteousness.

As in other things there is only one way to obtain the correct result. There is a precise formula for every achievement, an equation to solve every problem.

Then how can we suppose there are options in the way by which we obtain peace and life? To attempt to serve two masters or to dilute the formula of the Lord is but to invite disaster.

God has given us free agency. We may choose as we will. He does not restrict us. But he can and does tell us what results our deportment will bring. It comes back to the law of cause and effect. If we choose the right, we reap the harvest of goodness. If we choose the wrong, we invite degradation.

Intelligent as mortals seem to be, most have never learned that lesson, never profiting by others' mistakes nor by the advice of the truly wise. They blindly forge ahead, making the same mistakes countless others have made before them, and reaping the same harvest.

When will we be willing to accept God's direction instead of depending on our own poor judgment? Or why should we permit worldly circumstances to make our decisions for us; or leave those decisions to men whose views vary from revealed basic truth?

Inspired help is always available to us. Should we be ashamed to use it, although it may not have the gloss of worldly wisdom?

It was to perfect the Saints and guard them from "every wind of doctrine" that the Lord placed in his Church his apostles, prophets, pastors, and teachers. They are for the edifying of the Saints, teaching them both righteousness and the means of avoiding serious error.

God's ways are not man's ways. This we should learn. And we should have the good judgment to recognize that his ways always bring beneficial results.

People can be and often are honestly mistaken. But if we will seek the aid of our inspired leaders, we need never make serious errors.

What was it the wise man said?

"Trust in the Lord with all thine heart; and lean not to thine own understanding.

"In all thy ways acknowledge him, and he shall direct thy paths.

"Be not wise in thine own eyes: fear the Lord, depart from evil.

"It shall be health to thy navel, and marrow to thy bones.

"Honour the Lord with thy substance, and with the firstfruits of all thine increase:

"So shall thy barns be filled with plenty." (Prov. 3:5-10.)

Fundamental to making the right decisions, however, is an unhesitating acceptance of the reality of God.

But likewise we must be wise enough to admit and recognize the frightening fact that there is a personal devil who is our archenemy and who constantly entices us to do wrong.

Lehi taught that there must be an opposition in all things, otherwise we could not exercise our free agency. We would have no freedom of choice. (2 Ne. 2:11, 15.)

Knowing this, God provided that opposition, but made it abundantly clear to us that it is captained by the demon Lucifer.

Let us be reassured that God is real — a divine Person, our Eternal Father — and that he will direct us aright if we obey him.

But let us never forget that the devil is likewise real and diligent, and most surely will take over if we cross the line into his territory.

Chapter 3

The Devil Is Loose

The Lord speaks of Satan as "that old serpent," who is also referred to as the dragon seen by John the Revelator in his vision. He is Lucifer. He rebelled against both God the Father and Jesus the Savior, who is God's only divine Son.

Satan's rebellion was based upon selfishness, lust, covetousness and evil ambition. These are still his tools today. It is he who places wrongful ambition in the hearts of men, some of whom sell their own souls to achieve their ends. There are many Fausts in the world today, and Mephistopheles is forever on hand.

It is Satan who puts lust in the heart, lust for flesh, for money, for prestige. He is the father of all covetousness and lies, and selfishness is his stock in trade.

The characteristics which brought his downfall, he now seeks to implant in the hearts of every human being, so that they may fall even as he did.

Satan was a son of God, even as we all are. His position originally was one of glory and honor. He was an angel of God in great authority in the presence of God. (D&C 76:25.)

But his own greed destroyed his divine destiny. Blinded by his own selfishness, he turned against God.

"And there was war in heaven: Michael and his angels fought against the dragon [Lucifer]; and the dragon fought and his angels,

"And prevailed not; neither was their place found any more in heaven.

"And the great dragon was cast out, that old serpent, called the Devil, and Satan, which deceiveth the whole world: he was cast out into the earth, and his angels were cast out with him." (Rev. 12:7-9.)

When the Lord gave the Prophet Joseph Smith the revelation and vision recorded in section 76 of the Doctrine and Covenants, he spoke of the present-day war which Satan is waging against us, the Saints of God. It is a war to the death!

Significantly enough, the vision came to the Prophet as a great display of contrasts; the extreme of good, and the extreme of evil.

Joseph, with his companion Sidney Rigdon, had been given a view of the heavens in which "we beheld the glory of the Son on the right hand of the Father."

These humble young men were shown the holy angels and the sanctified ones who worship before the throne of God. And they saw the Christ! It was most impressive. Of it they wrote:

"And now, after the many testimonies which have been given of him, this is the testimony, last of all, which we give of him: That he lives!

"For we saw him, even on the right hand of God; and we heard the voice bearing record that he is the Only Begotten of the Father —

"That by him, and through him, and of him, the

worlds are and were created, and the inhabitants thereof are begotten sons and daughters unto God." (D&C 76:22-24.)

To what other men has such revelation and vision been given? It was stupendous, almost unparalleled, except possibly for the Prophet's first vision. It showed the glory of God, the reward of righteousness — the fruits of the Spirit.

But then came the contrast — a view of the fruits of lust. Of this the Prophet wrote:

"And this we saw also, and bear record, that an angel of God *who was in authority in the presence of God, who rebelled* against the Only Begotten Son whom the Father loved and who was in the bosom of the Father, was thrust down from the presence of God and the Son,

"And was called Perdition, for the heavens wept over him — he was Lucifer, a son of the morning.

"And we beheld, and lo, he is fallen! is fallen, even a son of the morning!

"And while we were yet in the Spirit, the Lord commanded us that we should write the vision; for we beheld Satan, that old serpent, even the devil, who rebelled against God, and sought to take the kingdom of our God and his Christ —

"Wherefore, he maketh war with the saints of God, and encompasseth them round about.

"And we saw a vision of the sufferings of those with whom he made war and overcame." (D&C 76:25-30. Italics added.)

After this vision, could Joseph and Sidney ever doubt the reality of God and the power of his Spirit, or the advisability of abiding in that Spirit?

And could they doubt the real existence of the devil and his power, or his evil intent to destroy the Saints of God?

The devil is loose in the world. He rages in the hearts of men, he lies and deceives and, as he did with Cain, he endeavors to tell modern people that they too may get gain if they kill and cheat and deceive.

But as it was with Cain so it is with us of today. Those who follow Cain's example will reap the harvest of Cain.

Chapter 4

Who Owns the Earth?

Since we are in a war with the devil, we should know that as the scriptures indicate, he is a liar and has been from the beginning.

One of his great sophistries is that he pretends to own the world, and all things in it, things to make us happy, and based on this falsehood he offers mankind thrills and excitement in following him.

As we know, the very opposite is true.

This great deception was attempted by Lucifer when he took the Lord "up into an exceeding high mountain, and sheweth him all the kingdoms of the world, and the glory of them; and saith unto him, All these things will I give thee, if thou wilt fall down and worship me." (Matt. 4:8-9.)

What a lie this was! He knew that he did not possess the world, but that it was the property of Jesus who had created it. For Lucifer to pretend to offer the Lord anything by way of earthly possessions was the greatest kind of effrontery.

This account prompted President Brigham Young to ask:

"Who owns the earth? Does the devil? No, he does not. He pretended to own it when the Savior was here and promised it all to him if he would fall down and worship him.

"But he did not own one foot of land. He was an intruder and still is. This earth belongs to him that framed and organized it, and it is expressly for his glory and the possession of those who love and serve him and keep his commandments." (*Discourses of Brigham Young,* Deseret Book Co., 1971 edition, ch. 6.)

But President Young indicated that under present conditions, Lucifer is most certainly using it.

When the devil promises by seductions that we can sin and get gain, he is lying to us as he did to Cain, and people who follow his wily ways must remember — but few of them do — that the Almighty has established a set of so-called natural laws which are as firm as the Rock of Gibraltar and with which we must deal whether we serve the Lord or whether we serve the devil.

How remarkably these laws are being displayed just now in the results of the use of tobacco, liquor, tea and coffee, to mention just a few. And think of the dreadful venereal diseases which are now in epidemic form in the world. And from whence do they come? From adultery! It is retribution in a most frightening way. And how well it proves the devil wrong!

It is almost ironic that certain forms of these diseases have no known cure whatsoever, that they last lifelong, and can break out years after exposure. Not even the devil heals them. Many of those who indulge in his infamous sexual traps go blind, are crippled, go insane — die. Syphilis is now one of the dreadful killer diseases.

But does the devil rescue his followers from such results? Never! He laughs at them for being so weak as to
fall into his trap. It was misery and misery alone he sought
for them, and that he heaps upon them heavily. He offers
fun, but what comes instead? Death and misery!

President Brigham Young said further on this point:

> "The difference between God and the devil is that
> God creates and organizes, while the whole study
> of the devil is to destroy. Every one that follows
> the evil inclinations of his own natural evil heart is
> going to destruction. . . . I pray you Latter-day
> Saints to live your religion." (*Discourses of Brigham
> Young,* p. 69.)

Again President Young, discoursing on the devil, said:

> "What then, is the mission of Satan, that common
> foe of all the children of men? It is to destroy and
> make desolate.
>
> "The devil delights in the work of destruction —
> to burn and lay waste and destroy the whole earth.
> He delights to convulse and throw into confusion the
> affairs of men, politically, religiously and morally,
> introducing war with its long train of dreadful con-
> sequences.
>
> "It is evil which causeth all these miseries and all
> deformity to come upon the inhabitants of the earth.
>
> "But that which is of God is pure, lovely, holy
> and full of all excellency and truth, no matter where
> it is found. . . .
>
> "The adversary presents his principles and argu-
> ments in the most approved style and in the most

winning tone, attended with the most graceful atti-
tudes.

"He is very careful to ingratiate himself into the
favor of the powerful and the influential of mankind,
uniting himself with popular parties, floating into
offices of trust and emolument by pandering to popular feeling, though it should seriously wrong and
oppress the innocent." (*Discourses of Brigham
Young*, p. 69.)

The President urged:

"Cease to mingle with the wicked. Many of our
elders seem to believe that Christ and Baal can yet be
made friends. How many times elders of Israel try
to make me fellowship the devil, or his imps, or his
servants; also try to make you fellowship your enemies, to amalgamate the feelings of the Saints and
the ungodly!

"It cannot be done. It never was done, and never
can be accomplished. Christ and Baal never can
be friends." (*Discourses of Brigham Young*, p. 71.)

The Prophet Joseph Smith was equally forceful in warning the Saints against the actual power of Satan, teaching
that it is he who inspires every evil teaching, every evil
thought, even in false religious creeds and organizations.

The Prophet then said that "the greatness of his pun-
ishment is that he shall not have a tabernacle." (*Teachings
of the Prophet Joseph Smith*, Deseret Book Co., p. 297.)

When we humans realize the reality of Satan, and the
vicious nature of his war against the Saints, we should raise
up our guard firmly against him.

The lesson of Cain must ever be in our minds. We
cannot sin and get gain.

Chapter 5

Satan Versus the Priesthood

The devil endeavored to destroy the Prophet Joseph in the Sacred Grove as the boy prophet sought the Lord for divine guidance.

But he attacks others of the Lord's servants also.

Elder LeGrand Richards of the Council of the Twelve relates a frightening experience which came to him in the Netherlands Mission. Said he:

"My companion and I had an unusual experience with evil spirits in the city of Amsterdam. We had held our morning meetings and had gone home to have lunch with a widow and her daughter and son. The daughter and son were members of the Church. The widow was not.

"After eating we tried to talk to her to see if we could not encourage her to become a member of the Church. She explained that she thought the Word of Wisdom was so hard to live.

"I explained to her that the Lord gave us the Word of Wisdom to free us from bad habits so that our bodies would be strong and healthy.

"Right at that time the evil spirits came upon her. From the sweet, lovely woman that she was she twisted her face and addressed me in the most sneering manner I had ever experienced. She said, 'Who are you?'

"I answered, 'I am a servant of the Lord.' She replied, 'So, you are a servant of the Lord.' Then she turned to her daughter and said, 'Who are you?' She replied, 'I am the daughter of the house.' 'So,' she replied, 'You are the daughter of the house.'

"Then turning to me again, she said, 'And who are you?' I replied that I was a servant of the Lord. Then she said, 'Well, if you are a servant of the Lord, then I have nothing to do here.'

"With that I called my two companions. We administered to her and rebuked the evil spirits. She fell limp and we carried her to the bedroom, put her on the bed and gave her cold water. In a short time she was the same sweet woman she had been before these spirits had entered her body.

"Her daughter explained that years earlier, before her father died, that her father and mother had come to America and had become interested in spiritualism. Since that time the spirits would not leave her mother alone. They would come and rap on the walls at night and disturb her. This was truly an unusual experience for us, and the first we had had of its character." (*Just to Illustrate,* Bookcraft, p. 96.)

One of the most notable of the contests between the devil and the ordained servants of the Lord came to Elder Heber C. Kimball of the Council of the Twelve and his associates during their mission in England.

It was during this mission that thousands of British people were converted to the Church, and began a migration from that land to Nauvoo when strength was sorely needed in the Church, for the devil was leading many of the American Saints into apostasy at this time.

This dreadful experience was as follows:

"Saturday evening," says Heber C. Kimball, "it was agreed that I should go forward and baptize, the next morning, in the river Ribble, which runs through Preston.

"By this time the adversary of souls began to rage, and he felt determined to destroy us before we had fully established the kingdom of God in that land, and the next morning I witnessed a scene of satanic power and influence which I shall never forget.

"Sunday, July 30th [1837], about daybreak, Elder Isaac Russell (who had been appointed to preach on the obelisk in Preston Square, that day), who slept with Elder Richards in Wilfred Street, came up to the third story, where Elder Hyde and myself were sleeping, and called out, 'Brother Kimball, I want you should get up and pray for me that I may be delivered from the evil spirits that are tormenting me to such a degree that I feel I cannot live long, unless I obtain relief.'

"I had been sleeping on the back of the bed. I immediately arose, slipped off at the foot of the bed, and passed around to where he was. Elder Hyde threw his feet out, and sat up in the bed, and we laid hands on him, I being mouth, and prayed that the Lord would have mercy on him, and rebuked the devil.

"While thus engaged, I was struck with great force by some invisible power, and fell senseless on the floor. The first thing I recollected was being supported by Elders Hyde and Richards, who were praying for me; Elder Richards having followed Russell up to my room.

"Elders Hyde and Richards then assisted me to get on the bed, but my agony was so great I could not endure it, and I arose, bowed my knees and prayed.

"I then arose and sat up on the bed, when a vision was opened to our minds, and we could distinctly see the evil spirits, who foamed and gnashed their teeth at us.

"We gazed upon them about an hour and a half (by Willard's watch). We were not looking towards the window, but towards the wall. Space appeared before us, and we saw the devils coming in legions, with their leaders, who came within a few feet of us.

"They came towards us like armies rushing to battle. They appeared to be men of full stature, possessing every form and feature of men in the flesh, who were angry and desperate; and I shall never forget the vindictive malignity depicted on their countenances as they looked me in the eye; and any attempt to paint the scene which then presented itself, or portray their malice and enmity, would be vain.

"I perspired exceedingly, my clothes becoming as wet as if I had been taken out of the river. I felt excessive pain, and was in the greatest distress for some time. I cannot even look back on the scene without feelings of horror; yet by it I learned the power of the adversary, his enmity against the servants of God, and got some understanding of the invisible world.

"We distinctly heard those spirits talk and express their wrath and hellish designs against us. However, the Lord delivered us from them, and blessed us exceedingly that day." (Orson F. Whitney, *Life of Heber C. Kimball,* Bookcraft, p. 135.)

Chapter 6

The War's Many Fronts

The devil maketh war with the Saints. But he likewise makes war against all other human beings, for he is not only interested in destroying the Church and the Saints, but seeks to gain for himself as many of the other children of Adam and Eve as he can, for they are all potential Saints.

One of the most frightening developments recently is the wildfire-like spread of actual devil worship. Cults of the devil have sprung up in America and Europe, made up of people who openly announce that they worship Lucifer and like it, that they are in league with him, and that they place themselves at his disposal to do whatever he directs them to do.

They have their seances going beyond anything known to the traditional spiritualist mediums. They receive from the depths of hell literal manifestations of the power of Satan. It is not imaginary. It is real. And it is modern. They give themselves over to him, make themselves available to him, and he quickly seizes upon this opportunity.

Newspapers have given wide publicity to devil worship. Many carry announcements of the times and places of their gatherings.

Evil spirits once again inhabit human bodies, even as in the days of Christ. Exorcists try to cast them out. A film which ran for months in the theaters exemplified the situation. But the exorcists are without divine power. Beelzebub puts on a show of casting out Beelzebub to further intrigue people.

But this is only one manifestation of his power. He is undermining and disabling the various Christian denominations which for centuries attempted to maintain truth and right, although their knowledge was limited and their divine authority nil.

But they did hold the line in virtue, in reading the scripture, in honest dealings, in advocating high principles of government.

But now they are weakening. Some of the smaller denominations are actually taking worldliness unto themselves. Some of their ministers have condoned the "new morality" which is promiscuity in its raw form.

Although the Bible is still our most widely distributed book, it is scantily read by the masses. Of what value is distribution if the pages are not scanned?

Church doors are being closed; congregations, ever growing smaller, are combining, hoping for strength which is still not there. Clergy are often more interested in politics than in religion. A priest became an inflammatory political advisor to a president, and was recalled by his church for "prayer and meditation." Another became a town mayor.

Crime in high places shocks millions. The order of the day seems to be the gratification of greediness. Governments in all parts of the western world are weaker today than at any time since the last world war, victims of creeping decadence. Public confidence is undermined. Mutual trust between officials is disappearing; accusations multiply with suspicions and denials.

In very recent years, since turmoil has taken over in the world, the governments of thirty-six nations have been overthrown; kings have been dethroned, premiers ousted, revolutionaries have taken over the reins of government. Dictatorship seems to be the order of the day.

Large business firms, long regarded as the soul of integrity, are now subjected to suits for alleged dishonesty and fraud.

The world is topsy-turvy. Money is losing its value. Honest hearts are wondering what is to come next? Many pray for the Millennium.

The world of flesh becomes manifest in the philosophical teachings of accredited scholars. Theories of anthropologists and other scientists are given more credence than scripture.

The Bible is treated as a myth. The account of Adam and Eve is scoffed at. Students in universities lose their faith in God as they accept atheistic teachings concerning the origin of man and the formation of the universe.

Philosophy not only discounts but displaces religion in many circles. Among so-called intellectuals it is embarrassing to even own a Bible or to open and scan its pages. Faith in God is taboo among such, for they teach that there is no God.

Look again at the chief characteristics of Satan. Note that they are deception (for he is the father of lies); covetousness; destruction of faith and virtue as well as all else that is good or tends toward godliness.

It is no wonder that the Savior said that only a few find the strait and narrow way, but that "wide is the gate, and broad is the way, that leadeth to destruction, and many there be which go in thereat." (Matt. 7:13.)

Paul told the Romans that "they that are in the flesh

cannot please God. . . . Now if any man have not the Spirit of Christ, he is none of his." (Rom. 8:8-9.)

In the very dawn of human life upon the earth, Adam taught his children the facts of true religion. But Satan was quick to come among them, saying, "Believe it not," and they believed it not. Many of Adam's children then loved Satan more than God. Dare we of today follow their destructive pattern, we who know of the gospel plan?

Chapter 7

The Power of Witchcraft

President Joseph F. Smith was outspoken concerning devil cults, the power of Satan to influence the lives of people, the casting of a "curse" upon some hapless individuals, the use of spiritualistic methods, and the like.

He was a prophet of God. He spoke by the power of his office. He knew of the deceitfulness of Satan, but he also knew of the direct light and direction of the Holy Spirit.

It was out of this wisdom that he said:

> "After all the horrors, persecutions, and cruelties that have been brought about by the senseless belief in witchcraft, it seems strange in this age of enlightenment that men or women, especially those who have received the gospel, can be found anywhere who believe in such a pernicious superstition.
>
> "The Bible and history alike conclusively brand this superstition as a child of evil. In ancient times, God required the Israelites to drive the Canaanites from their land, and witchcraft was one of the crimes which he laid at the door of the Canaanites, and for which they were adjudged unworthy of the land which they possessed.
>
> "Witchcraft has not infrequently been the last resort of the evildoer. Men bereft of the Spirit of God,

when the voice of the Lord has ceased to warn them, have frequently resorted to witchcraft, in the endeavor to learn that which Heaven withheld; and the people of God from very early days to the present have been troubled with superstitions and evil-minded persons who have resorted to divination and kindred devices for selfish purposes, and scheming designs. In the Middle Ages it rested like a nightmare upon all Christendom.

"Let it not be forgotten that the evil one has great power in the earth, and that by every possible means he seeks to darken the minds of men, and then offers them falsehood and deception in the guise of truth. Satan is a skillful imitator, and as genuine gospel truth is given the world in ever-increasing abundance, so he spreads the counterfeit coin of false doctrine.

"Beware of his spurious currency, it will purchase for you nothing but disappointment, misery and spiritual death. The 'father of lies' he has been called, and such an adept liar has he become, through the ages of practice in his nefarious work, that were it possible he would deceive the very elect.

"Those who turn to soothsayers and wizards for their information are invariably weakening their faith. When men began to forget the God of their fathers who had declared himself in Eden and subsequently to the later patriarchs, they accepted the devil's substitute and made for themselves gods of wood and stone. It was thus that the abominations of idolatry had their origin.

"The gifts of the Spirit and the powers of the holy Priesthood are of God, they are given for the blessing of the people, for their encouragement, and for the strengthening of their faith.

"This Satan knows full well, therefore he seeks by imitation-miracles to blind and deceive the children of God. Remember what the magicians of Egypt accomplished in their efforts to deceive Pharaoh as to the divinity of the mission of Moses and Aaron.

"John the Revelator saw in, vision the miracle-working power of the evil one. Note his words. 'And I beheld another beast coming up out of the earth; . . . and he doeth great wonders, so that he maketh fire come down from heaven on the earth in the sight of men, and deceiveth them that dwell on the earth by the means of those miracles,' etc. (Rev. 13:11, 13-14.)

"Further, John saw three unclean spirits whom he describes as 'the spirits of devils, working miracles.' (Rev. 16:13-14.)

"That the power to work wonders may come from an evil source is declared by Christ in his prophecy regarding the great judgment: 'Many will say to me in that day, Lord, Lord, have we not prophesied in thy name? and in thy name have cast out devils? and in thy name done many wonderful works? And then will I profess unto them, I never knew you: depart from me, ye that work iniquity.' (Matt. 7:22-23.)

"The danger and power for evil in witchcraft is not so much in the witchcraft itself as in the foolish credulence that superstitious people give to the claims made in its behalf. It is outrageous to believe that the devil can hurt or injure an innocent man or woman, especially if they are members of the Church of Christ — without that man or woman has faith that he or she can be harmed by such an influence and by such means. If they entertain such an idea, then they are liable to succumb to their own superstitions. There is no power in witchcraft itself, only as it is believed in and accepted. . . .

"It is really astonishing that there should be any to believe in these absurdities. No man or woman who enjoys the Spirit of God and the influence and power of the holy Priesthood can believe in these superstitious notions, and those who do, will lose, indeed have lost, the influence of the Spirit of God and of the Priesthood, and are become subject to the witchery of Satan, who is constantly striving to draw away the Saints from the true way, if not by the dissemination of such nonsense, then by other insidious methods.

"One individual cannot place an affliction upon another in the way that these soothsayers would have the people believe. It is a trick of Satan to deceive men and women, and to draw them away from the Church and from the influence of the Spirit of God, and the power of his holy Priesthood, that they may be destroyed.

"These peepstone-men and women are inspired by the devil, and are the real witches, if any such there be.

"Witchcraft, and all kindred evils, are solely the creations of the superstitious imaginations of men and women who are steeped in ignorance, and derive their power over people from the devil, and those who submit to this influence are deceived by him.

"Unless they repent, they will be destroyed. There is absolutely no possibility for a person who enjoys the Holy Spirit of God even to believe that such influences can have any effect upon him.

"The enjoyment of the Holy Spirit is absolute proof against all influences of evil: you never can obtain that Spirit by seeking diviners, and men and women who 'peep and mutter.' That is obtained by imposition of hands by the servants of God, and retained by right living.

"If you have lost it, repent and return to God, and for your salvation's sake and for the sake of your children, avoid the emissaries of Satan who 'peep and mutter' and who would lead you down to darkness and death.

"It is impossible for anyone possessing the spirit of the gospel and having the power of the holy Priesthood to believe in or be influenced by any power of necromancy." (*Gospel Doctrine*, Deseret Book Co., pp. 374-378.)

Chapter 8

The Ancient Dissonants

One of the devil's favorite pastimes seems to be the organization of dissonant religious groups into cults and separatist churches of their own.

From the beginning of time this has been true. When Adam taught the true religion to his family, the devil came and said, "Believe it not," and many believed it not.

But they were not left without religion. Satan provided his own, in various forms. The pagan religions go back to the dawn of history, and they have been in wide variety, ranging from worship of the sun, moon and stars, to fire worship and adoration of the rivers and lakes. Among the worst were those in which human beings were sacrificed, to undefinable deities, and this was done in both hemispheres.

Even Moses had his opponents, who fostered apostate cults until the coming of Christ.

It is well remembered that the Savior said to the cultists of his day: "Did not Moses give you the law, and yet none of you keepeth the law?" (John 7:19.)

And because they had departed so far from the law, they sought to kill the Savior when he preached his pure doctrine, and eventually they did. He became a victim of their religious intolerance and apostasy.

There was no religious unity among the Jews when Jesus came. Some of the apostate cults in existence in his day were the well-known Pharisees and Sadducees, of course. But there were also the Essenes, believed to have written the Dead Sea scrolls. There were the Zealots, a religious anti-Roman cult, and there were the Hellenists. These latter were an interesting lot.

About four hundred years before Christ, Alexander the Great sought to conquer the world. As a result of his wars, Greek culture was imposed upon his satellite nations, including Palestine.

Strong resistance met this movement among the Jews, even divided as they were among their own cults. On this they united. But the movement grew, encouraged as it was first by Greek rule and then by Roman rule. It was known as the Hellenist group or party because it sought to Hellenize or impose Greek culture upon all nations including the Jews.

The Hellenists accepted many of the apostate inroads made into the Mosaic law but also rejected Jewish temple worship. They were much like the Essenes in this respect, for they shut the temple out of their lives also.

When the Savior came, these apostate cults persisted. He taught his own true doctrine, but although he attracted thousands as he fed them loaves and fishes, by the time of Pentecost, following his atonement, only 120 people came to the meeting of the Saints in Jerusalem.

However, many others joined the Church afterward. Three thousand were baptized in one day. But conflicts arose early. There was serious disagreement between the Jews and the Greeks who had joined the Church, and had brought in the Hellenist influence. They found it hard to divest themselves of Greek philosophy.

There were now many Greeks in Palestine, brought in

by government and commerce as a means of helping to Hellenize the area. Greek became a popular language there also, it being the language of "culture." This is why the early New Testament books were provided in that tongue.

Following the death of the apostles, division spread rapidly within Christianity. Historians say that within a hundred years of Christ there were as many as thirty different denominations.

It is a great mistake to assume that there was but one and only one Christian Church until Constantine's day and beyond that to the schism forming the Greek Orthodox Catholic Church about a thousand years after Christ.

Christianity was widely splintered, almost from its beginning.

At the time of the destruction of Jerusalem in A.D. 70 most of the cults were broken up as the Jews were scattered hither and yon. This was the great opportunity of the Hellenists, however, for they were sponsored by the Romans, who continued to foster Greek culture wherever they went. So beginning at that time, Hellenism became the dominant sect of Christianity. But many others still persisted for years.

Among the sects of Christians which developed into denominations in that early day were:

The Judaeo-Christians who tried to Judaize the Christian religion by introducing Mosaic rituals, including circumcision.

The Millennarianists.

The Encratites, an austere sect who, out of abhorrence for wine, used water instead of wine in the sacrament of the Lord's Supper.

The Ebionites.

The Gnostics, who rejected both Jehovah and the Mosaic law.

The Archontics, who believed in seven heavens, each one presided over by a Prince; they also believed in the Supreme Mother of Heaven, a faith condemned in Jeremiah chapters 7 and 44.

The Coptics, who are still prominent in Egypt.

The Syriac Christians, centered in Damascus, at that time one of the principal though paganistic cities in the Middle East.

The Mandaeans, a baptist cult, who opposed the rise of sprinkling as a mode of baptism.

The Manichaeans.

The Quartodecimans.

The Hellenists, and others.

Since the Hellenists gained preference after the destruction of Jerusalem, being favored by the Romans themselves, this was the group known to the Romans in the time of Constantine.

The main centers of the Church in the time of Constantine were at Alexandria in Egypt and at Constantinople.

With the destruction of much of the city of Jerusalem in the Roman wars, and with the scattering of the Jews, that city now lost its prominence in the Christian Church. The few Christians who returned there after the wars were no longer influential.

The Church was definitely an eastern church. Rome at this time was hardly heard of, so far as the Church was concerned, and counted for little in Christianity until two more centuries had gone by, and then only through political influence.

The great Council of Nicaea was of course an eastern council, not even attended by representation from Rome.

So Christianity was an eastern church in those days and was controlled largely by the Hellenists, who depended on Greek philosophy and the power of Roman politics.

It will be remembered that both Arius and Athanasius were Greek philosophers who were trained in the Greek schools of philosophy in Alexandria.

It was they who debated the nature of God at the Council of Nicaea, in Asia Minor, a conflict ultimately decided by the non-Christian Constantine. Its outcome was another victory for the Hellenists and their philosophers.

The Nicene Creed was based largely on their philosophy, and had little to do with true scriptural doctrine.

An interesting discussion in this regard is provided by the editors of the *Twentieth Century Encyclopedia of Catholicism,* volume 17, pages 117 to 137.

On page 118 we read:

"What would have happened if St. Athanasius had not made use of Greek thought as well as scripture? . . . From the religious point of view Christianity could never have overridden the differences between Greek and Barbarian, Jew and Gentile, if it had remained Jewish in its way of thought, if it had not acquired through contact with the Greek genius that suppleness which enabled it to reach all systems of thought."

On page 123 of the same volume appears:

"Greek theology was well adapted to become a marvelous guide to express for man the depth of his relationship with God."

Then on page 124 we have:

"St. Augustine showed that the Holy Spirit proceeds from the Father and the Son — that the Father and the Son are entranced with love for each other, that they meet in a love which is common to them both *and that love is the Holy Spirit.*" (Italics added.)

On page 131 we read:

"This love is the Holy Spirit of whom St. Bernard said that he is the kiss exchanged between the Father and the Son."

To this extreme did Greek philosophy distort the simple Christian doctrine of the Godhead.

Could anyone doubt that the devil would delight in thus confusing the minds of people so that they could not tell what or whom they worshipped?

Divisions grew once again. Not even these Hellenists could agree among themselves, as is evident in the rupture which developed about A.D. 1000 with the creation of the Greek Orthodox Catholic Church.

The conflict among the Greek philosophers, which had an indelible effect on Christianity, is well described by Saint Augustine in his book, *The City of God,* which was written about A.D. 410.

Although he wrote concerning his associate philosophers in general, showing the wide disparity of their views, he freely acknowledges the effect of their debates on Christian dogma.

He mentions that there were 288 different schools of Greek philosophy and adds that "each was the inventor of its own dogmas and opinions" and that there were "very many of them whose love of truth severed them from their teachers or fellow-disciples that they might strive for what they thought was the truth whether it was or not."

Augustine then continues:

"Yet did not each gather disciples to follow his sect? Indeed in the conspicuous and well-known porch, the gymnasia, in gardens, in public places and private, they openly strove in bands each for his own opinion; some asserting there was one world, others innumerable worlds; some that this world had a beginning, others that it had not; some that it would perish, others that it would exist always; some that it was governed by the divine mind, others by chance and accident; some that souls are immortal, others that they are mortal, and of those who asserted their immortality, some said they transmigrated through beasts, others that it was by no means so; while those who asserted their mortality, some said they perished immediately after the body; others that they survived either a little while or a longer time, but not always."

And then the learned Augustine goes on:

"Now, what people, senate, power or public dignity of the impious city has ever taken care to judge between all these and other well-nigh innumerable dissensions of the philosophers, approving and accepting some, and disapproving and rejecting others? . . .

"Even if some true things were said, yet falsehoods were uttered with the same license, so that such a city has not amiss received the title of the mystic Babylon. Nor does it matter to the devil its king how they wrangle among themselves, in contradictory errors, since all alike deservedly belong to him on account of their great and varied impiety." (See *City of God*, pp. 648-671.)

Since the Hellenists had taken over Christianity so extensively, and since Hellenism fostered this kind of Greek philosophical debate, what possible chance had pure Christianity to survive?

As Augustine himself said, the devil was their king and didn't mind how much wrangling went on among their contradictory errors. But the debates obscured and destroyed the truth.

Was not all of this splintering of Christian groups pleasing to Satan? Since Christ taught unity, "even as my Father and I are one," is there anything that would please Lucifer more than this growing and constant disunity among the professed believers in Christ?

The Greeks debated the nature of God in time of Plato, 400 B.C. Their philosophers still debated the same question in the time of Arius and Athanasius, and were at it even in A.D. 400 at the time of Augustine, another Greek philosopher, who is regarded as the strongest of the early "fathers" although he came into the ministry from the schools of philosophy and from a life of licentiousness in his earlier years.

But the end was not yet. Next came the Protestant reformation with additional denominations and creeds. And still the end has not come.

At the present time there are 250 different Christian denominations listed in the catalogue of the National Council of the Churches of Christ in America.

Among them are four different Adventist groups; twenty-seven Baptist groups; nine churches of "The Brethren"; and fourteen different groups of the Church of God.

Among the Catholics are the Catholic Apostolic Church, the Roman Catholics, the Greek Orthodox Catholics, the Liberal Catholics, the Old Catholics (of which there are five subdivisions) and the Polish National Catholics.

There are twelve Evangelical churches, eight organizations of Quakers or Friends, nine denominations of Lutherans, twelve Mennonites, seven so-called Reformed churches, nineteen denominations of Methodists, twelve Pentecostal Assembly groups, and nine versions of Presbyterians.

These are merely the larger groups.

It represents multiple division, the opposite of Christ's teaching, but the exact procedure of Satan, who would nullify Christianity by conflicts within its various groups.

It is no wonder that Jesus taught the Nephites:

"There shall be no disputations among you, as there have hitherto been; neither shall there be disputations among you concerning the points of my doctrine, as there have hitherto been.

"For verily, verily I say unto you, he that hath the spirit of contention is not of me, *but is of the devil,* who is the father of contention, and he stirreth up the hearts of men to contend with anger, one with another.

"Behold, this is not my doctrine, to stir up the hearts of men with anger, one against another; but this is my doctrine, that such things should be done away." (3 Ne. 11:28-30. Italics added.)

Chapter 9

The Modern Dissonants

Satan did all in his power to destroy the work of the Prophet Joseph Smith. Not only did he attack him in the Sacred Grove; not only did he raise enemies against him who made many false charges and had him put in prison, but the devil likewise caused disruption within the Church itself.

Close associates of the Prophet in his holy ministry turned against him. Some established churches of their own. Six of the apostles betrayed him; some joined the forces of martyrdom.

The witnesses to the Book of Mormon left his side; Sidney Rigdon, his close confidant and friend in the First Presidency, abandoned him when persecution became more severe.

But God was with the Prophet and his work. He never would allow Satan to overcome it and never will. The Church goes on and prospers.

Nevertheless, there are still dissonant groups, some teaching alleged new revelation, as they think it to be; others engaging in unlawful marriage practices, some living a communal life. But all are deceived by Satan, and all seek to lead the Saints astray.

Did not the devil declare war against the Saints? If he can mislead them with false doctrines and false teachers, will he not do so? The Savior warned against such things in his ministry on earth, and he still does.

There are several splinter groups even today, led by men making false claims to new revelation, declaring the Church to have gone astray, or saying that we observe only a part of the gospel and reject the rest.

One group, led by a woman, claims that the fall of Adam was a mistake, and that death is not necessary. The suggestion is that if people will but follow her they will go on into immortality without the process of either death or resurrection. In this way she repudiates the Lord's atonement, and becomes anti-Christ.

Another group claims that the modern presence of the Melchizedek Priesthood is a mistake, that only the Aaronic Priesthood should be on earth at this time. The claim results from an alleged vision of John the Revelator who is said to have brought the Aaronic Priesthood back to earth about thirty years ago. Why it was not John the Baptist, or even Aaron after whom this priesthood was named, is a mystery. What did the Revelator have to do with the priesthood of Aaron? Oh, consistency!

But the claimants rewrote portions of the Doctrine and Covenants, changing the revelations to suit their own convenience. They attempt to live a communal-type life.

And then there are the three groups — all antagonistic to each other — who advocate the present practice of plural marriage in accordance with ancient law.

It is a fact that plural marriage was lived by some anciently. There were two kinds of plural marriage approved of God in biblical times. One was a type of "church welfare program" to care for widows, to keep them from becoming a public charge.

This is referred to in Matthew 22:23-30, where occurs the account of the woman who had seven husbands.

It is mentioned also in Deuteronomy 25:5, where it is given as a law to ancient Israel by Moses. Mention is made of it also in Genesis 38:8, long before the Mosaic law was given.

This form of plural marriage was a means of keeping a widow from destitution. If her husband died, the next of kin would marry the woman and support her. The entire story of Ruth in the Bible is based upon this law, and Jesus came through her lineage. So this kind of marriage was provided by the Lord under these special circumstances.

Then in cases of sterility, such as with Abraham and Sarah, again polygamy was permitted if agreed to by the Lord.

But as the Book of Mormon so clearly points out — plural marriage was always forbidden unless the Lord himself decreed it and permitted it. Says Jacob in the Book of Mormon:

> "David and Solomon truly had many wives and concubines, which thing was abominable before me, saith the Lord. . . .
>
> "Wherefore, I the Lord God will not suffer that this people shall do like unto them of old.
>
> "Wherefore, my brethren, hear me, and hearken to the word of the Lord: For there shall not any man among you have save it be one wife; and concubines he shall have none;
>
> "For I, the Lord God, delight in the chastity of women. And whoredoms are an abomination before me; thus saith the Lord of Hosts.

"Wherefore, this people shall keep my commandments, saith the Lord of Hosts, or cursed be the land for their sakes.

"For if I will, saith the Lord of Hosts, raise up seed unto me, I will command my people; otherwise they shall hearken unto these things." (Jac. 2:24-26, 30.)

Why was plural marriage practiced by the Latter-day Saints? Only about 4 percent of them ever entered into this form of matrimony, but why did even they?

When the apostle Peter spoke, as is recorded in Acts 3, he referred to the second coming of the Savior and indicated that this great event will not take place until the time of the restoration of all things spoken by the Lord through his prophets from the beginning of the world.

All things were to be restored!

Would this include plural marriage? It did, and hence section 132 of the Doctrine and Covenants was given. In verses 40 and 45 of that section, as he speaks of plural marriage to Joseph Smith, the Lord refers to it as part of the restoration of all things.

The Prophet Joseph did not wish to enter polygamy. It was farthest from his mind. But he was the restorer, and through him "all things" must be restored. Hence under the persuasion of the Lord, he accepted it. This is why there was polygamy among the Mormons.

When the Saints migrated to the Rocky 'Mountains, and a limited number began the practice of plural marriage, enemies appeared immediately. Eventually the powers of the United States government were martialed to crush this new development.

Laws were enacted in Congress and upheld by the Supreme Court, banning plural marriage in America. The

Church was committed to honor, uphold and sustain the law.

The leaders were in a great quandary. They accepted persecution while awaiting the word of the Lord; some went to prison; Church properties were seized, the temples were taken over by government agents and all ordinance work for the living and the dead was stopped.

President Wilford Woodruff, the inspired servant of God, sought direction from heaven. He would do only what God commanded him to do, regardless of opposition.

As a result of his inquiries, he received visions and revelations on the subject, providing the instructions he needed. The Manifesto was the result, issued to the Church October 6, 1890. It prohibited further plural marriages in the Church. The Saints, in general conference assembled, accepted it as having come from God through their prophet.

It is now published in the Doctrine and Covenants as follows:

"OFFICIAL DECLARATION

"To Whom it may Concern:

"Press dispatches having been sent for political purposes, from Salt Lake City, which have been widely published, to the effect that the Utah Commission, in their recent report to the Secretary of the Interior, allege that plural marriages are still being solemnized and that forty or more such marriages have been contracted in Utah since last June or during the past year, also that in public discourses the leaders of the Church have taught, encouraged and urged the continuance of the practice of polygamy —

"I, therefore, as President of the Church of Jesus Christ of Latter-day Saints, do hereby, in the most solemn manner, declare that these charges are false.

We are not teaching polygamy or plural marriage, nor permitting any person to enter into its practice, and I deny that either forty or any other number of plural marriages have during that period been solemnized in our Temples or in any other place in the Territory.

"One case has been reported, in which the parties allege that the marriage was performed in the Endowment House, in Salt Lake City, in the Spring of 1889, but I have not been able to learn who performed the ceremony; whatever was done in this matter was without my knowledge. In consequence of this alleged occurrence the Endowment House was, by my instructions, taken down without delay.

"Inasmuch as laws have been enacted by Congress forbidding plural marriages, which laws have been pronounced constitutional by the court of last resort, I hereby declare my intention to submit to those laws, and to use my influence with the members of the Church over which I preside to have them do likewise.

"There is nothing in my teachings to the Church or in those of my associates, during the time specified, which can be reasonably construed to inculcate or encourage polygamy; and when any Elder of the Church has used language which appeared to convey any such teaching, he has been promptly reproved. And I now publicly declare that my advice to the Latter-day Saints is to refrain from contracting any marriage forbidden by the law of the land.

"Wilford Woodruff

"President of the Church of Jesus Christ of Latter-day Saints."

Afterward, President Woodruff gave the following as part of an address in Logan, Utah, November 1, 1891, at the Cache Stake conference. It was quoted as follows in the *Deseret News* of November 7, 1891 (italics have been added):

"I made some remarks last Sunday at Brigham City upon the same principle, revelation. Read the life of Brigham Young and you can hardly find a revelation that he had wherein he said 'Thus saith the Lord;' but the Holy Ghost was with him; he taught by inspiration and by revelation; but with one exception he did not give those revelations in the form that Joseph did; for they were not written and given as revelations and commandments to the Church in the words and name of the Savior.

"Joseph said, 'Thus saith the Lord' almost every day of his life, in laying the foundation of this work. But those who followed him have not deemed it always necessary to say, 'Thus saith the Lord;' yet they have led the people by the power of the Holy Ghost.

"If you want to know what that is, read the first six verses of the 68th Section of the Book of Doctrine and Covenants, where the Lord told Orson Hyde, Luke Johnson, Lyman Johnson, and William E. McLellin to go out and preach the gospel to people as they were moved upon by the Holy Ghost:

" 'And whatsoever they shall speak when moved upon by the Holy Ghost shall be scripture, shall be the word of the Lord, shall be the mind of the Lord, shall be the voice of the Lord, and the power of God unto salvation.'

"It is by that power that we have led Israel. By that power President Young presided over and led the Church. By the same power President John Taylor presided over and led the Church. And that is the way I have acted according to the best of my ability, in that capacity.

"I do not want the Latter-day Saints to understand that the Lord is not with us, and that He is not giving revelations to us; for He is giving us revelation, and will give us revelation until this scene is wound up.

"I have had some revelations of late, and very important ones to me, and I will tell you what the Lord has said to me. Let me bring your minds to what is termed the Manifesto.

"The Lord has told me by revelation that there are many members of the Church throughout Zion who are sorely tried in their hearts because of that Manifesto. And also because of the testimony of the Presidency of the Church and the Apostles before the Master in Chancery.

"Since I received that revelation I have heard of many who are tried in these things, though I had not heard of any before that particularly. Now, the Lord has commanded me to do one thing, and I fulfilled that commandment at the conference at Brigham City last Sunday, and I will do the same here today.

"The Lord has told me to ask the Latter-day Saints a question, and He also told me that if they would listen to what I said to them and answer the question put to them, by the spirit and power of God, they would all answer alike, and they would all believe alike with regard to this matter.

"The question is this: 'Which is the wisest course for the Latter-day Saints to pursue — to continue to attempt to practice plural marriage, with the laws of the land against it and the opposition of 60,000,000 people and at the cost of the confiscation and loss of all the temples, and the stopping of all the ordinances therein, both for the living and the dead, and the imprisonment of the First Presidency and Twelve and the heads of families in the Church, and the confiscation of all personal property of the people (all of which of themselves would not stop the practice), or after doing and suffering what we have through our adherence to this principle to cease the practice and submit to the law and through doing so, to leave the Prophets, Apostles, and fathers at home, so that they can instruct the people and attend to the duties of the Church, and also leave the temples in the hands of the Saints, so that they can attend to the ordinances of the gospel, both for the living and for the dead?'

"The Lord showed me by vision and revelation exactly what would take place if we did not stop this practice. If we had not stopped, it would have had no use for Brother Merrill, for Brother Adlofson, for Brother Roskelley, for Brother Leishman, or for any of the men in this temple at Logan; for all ordinances would be stopped throughout the land of Zion.

"Confusion would reign throughout Israel, and many men would be made prisoners. This trouble would have come upon the whole Church, and we would have been compelled to stop the practice.

"Now, the question is, whether it should be stopped in this manner, or in the way the Lord has manifested to us, and leave our Prophets and Apostles and fathers free men, and the temples in the hands of the people, so that the dead may be redeemed. A large number has already been delivered from the prison house in the spirit world, by this people, and shall the work go on or stop?

"This is the question I lay before the Latter-day Saints. You have to judge for yourselves. I want you to answer it for yourselves. I shall not answer it; but I say to you that is exactly the condition we as a people would have been in had we not taken the course we have.

"I know there are a good many men and probably some leading men, in this Church who have been tried and felt as though President Woodruff has lost the spirit of God and was about to apostatize.

"Now, I want you to understand that he has not lost the Spirit nor is he about to apostatize. The Lord is with him, and with this people.

"He has told me exactly what to do and what the result would be if we did not do it.

"I have been called upon by friends outside of the Church and urged to take some steps with regard to this matter. They knew the course which the Government was determined to take. This feeling has also been manifested more or less by the members of the Church.

"I saw exactly what would come to pass if there was not something done. I have had this spirit upon me for a long time.

"But I want to say this: *I should have let all the Temples go out of our hands; I should have gone to prison myself; and let every other man go there; had not the God of heaven commanded me to do what I did do and when the hour came that I was commanded to do that, it was all clear to me.*

"I went before the Lord, and I wrote what the Lord told me to write. I laid it before my brethren — such strong men as Brother George Q. Cannon, Brother Joseph F. Smith, and the Twelve Apostles.

I might as well undertake to turn an army with banners out of its course as to turn them out of a course that they considered to be right. No. Why? Because they were moved upon by the Spirit of God and by the revelations of Jesus Christ to do it. . . ." (Italics added.)

President Woodruff made a further statement on the subject during the sixth session of the dedicatory services for the Salt Lake Temple in April 1893, in which he said:

"I feel disposed to say something upon the Manifesto. To begin with, I will say that this work was like a mountain upon me. I saw by the inspiration of Almighty God what lay before this people, and I knew that something had to be done to ward off the blow that I saw impending.

"But I should have let come to pass what God showed me by revelation and vision; I should have lived in the flesh and permitted these things to come to pass; I should have let this temple go into the hands of our enemies; I should have let every temple be confiscated by the hands of the wicked; I should have permitted our personal property to have been confiscated by our enemies; I should have seen this people — prophets and apostles, driven by the hands of their enemies, and our wives and children scattered to the four winds of heaven — I should have seen all this, *had not Almighty God commanded me to do what I did.*

"Did any of you ever know Joseph Smith, or Brigham Young, or John Taylor? Did you know of what material they were made? Was there a man on God's footstool that could have moved them to the right or the left from anything that they felt inspired to do? No.

"Here are George Q. Cannon, Joseph F. Smith, and these Twelve Apostles. I want to ask you if Wilford Woodruff could have done anything that the men would have accepted, in performing the work that was done, that pained the hearts of all Israel, except by the spirit and power of God? No.

"I would just as soon have thought of moving the foundations of this world as to have taken any course to move these men only by the revelations of God. When that Manifesto was given they accepted of it. Why?

"Because they had the Spirit of God for themselves; they knew for themselves it was right. It was passed also before ten thousand Latter-day Saints and there was not a solitary hand lifted against that edict. They also had the spirit of revelation for themselves.

"Now I will tell you what was manifest to me, and what the Son of God performed in this thing. The Lord has never yet taken from Lucifer, the Son of the Morning, his agency. He still holds it, and will hold it until he is bound with the keys of death and hell. The devil still has power; and the Son of God knew full well if something was not done in order to check this, all these things which I have referred to would have come to pass.

"Yes, I saw by vision and revelation this temple in the hands of the wicked; I saw our city in the hands of the wicked; I saw every temple in these valleys in the hands of the wicked; I saw great destruction among the people.

"And these things would have come to pass, as God Almighty lives, had not that Manifesto been given. Therefore, the Son of God felt disposed to have that thing presented to the Church and to the world, for purposes in His own mind.

"The Lord had decreed the establishment of Zion. The Lord had decreed the finishing of this Temple. He had decreed that the salvation of the living and the dead should be given in these valleys of the mountains.

"And God Almighty decreed that the devil should not have the power to thwart it. If you can understand that, that is the key to it."

So polygamy was given to the Latter-day Saints by the Lord as part of the restoration of all things, and now it was taken away by the Lord. In both instances — the giving of this practice and its discontinuance — it was a divine act. It was not of man.

Chapter 10

Further Pronouncements

There were a few of the members of the Church who would not accept the Manifesto of President Woodruff. Misunderstandings occurred, false rumors were circulated.

In view of these conditions President Lorenzo Snow, who succeeded President Woodruff in the presidency of the Church, published the following statement in the *Deseret News* on January 8, 1900:

"POLYGAMY AND UNLAWFUL COHABITATION

"From the reading of the various editorials and articles of the public press it is evident that there is much misconstruction and misunderstanding as to the present attitude of our Church respecting the subject of polygamy and unlawful cohabitation; and, believing that many good and conscientious people have been misled and much adverse criticism occasioned thereby, I feel it but just to both 'Mormons' and non-'Mormons' to state that, in accordance with the Manifesto of the late President Wilford Woodruff, dated September 24th, 1890, which was presented to and unanimously accepted by our General Conference on the 6th of October, 1890, the Church has positively abandoned the practice of polygamy, or the solemnization of plural marriages, in this and every other state, and that no member or officer thereof has any authority whatever to perform a plural marriage or enter into such a relation.

"Nor does the Church advise or encourage unlawful cohabitation on the part of any of its members. If, therefore, any member disobeys the law, either as to polygamy or unlawful cohabitation, he must bear his own burden or in other words, be answerable to the tribunals of the land for his own action pertaining thereto.

"With a sincere desire that the position of our Church as to polygamy and unlawful cohabitation may be better understood, and with best wishes for the welfare and happiness of all, this statement was made, and is respectfully commended to the careful consideration of the public generally.

"Lorenzo Snow

"President of the Church of Jesus Christ of Latter-day Saints.
"Salt Lake City, January 8, 1900."

Nevertheless there were still some who held that since the Edmunds law was an American law, it could not prevent the practice of plural marriage in Canada and Mexico.

To forestall this, another statement came from the First Presidency, this time during the regime of President Joseph F. Smith. It was as follows:

"PLURAL MARRIAGES FORBIDDEN —

Official Statement —

"Inasmuch as there are numerous reports in circulation that plural marriages have been entered into

contrary to the official declaration of President
Woodruff, of September 24, 1890, commonly called
the Manifesto, which was issued by President Woodruff and adopted by the Church at its general conference, October 6, 1890, which forbade any marriages
violative of the law of the land; I, Joseph F. Smith,
President of the Church of Jesus Christ of Latter-day
Saints, hereby affirm and declare that no such marriages have been solemnized with the sanction, consent or knowledge of the Church of Jesus Christ of
Latter-day Saints, and I hereby announce that all
such marriages are prohibited, and if any officer or
member of the Church shall assume to solemnize or
enter into any such marriage he will be deemed in
transgression against the Church and will be liable
to be dealt with according to the rules and regula-
tions thereof, and excommunicated therefrom.

"Joseph F. Smith

"President of the Church of Jesus Christ of
Latter-day Saints."
(*Conference Report,* April 1904, p. 75.)

"FURTHER STATEMENT.

"We have announced in previous conferences, as
it was announced by President Woodruff, as it was
announced by President Snow, and as it was re-
announced by me and my brethren and confirmed by
the Church of Jesus Christ of Latter-day Saints,
plural marriages have ceased in the Church.

"There isn't a man today in this Church or any-
where else, outside of it, who has authority to solemnize a plural marriage — not one!

"There is no man or woman in the Church of
Jesus Christ of Latter-day Saints who is authorized

to contract a plural marriage. It is not permitted, and we have been endeavoring to the utmost of our ability to prevent men from being led by some designing person into an unfortunate condition that is forbidden by the conferences, and by the voice of the Church, a condition that has to some extent, at least, brought reproach upon the people.

"I want to say that we have been doing all in our power to prevent it or to stop it; and in order that we might do this, we have been seeking, to our utmost, to find men who have been the agents and the cause of leading people into it. We find it very difficult to trace them but when we do find them, and can prove it upon them, we will deal with them as we have dealt with others that we have been able to find." (President Joseph F. Smith, *Conference Report,* April 1911, p. 8.)

Chapter 11

Spurious Revelation

To justify their own rebellion, certain recalcitrant brethren devised a scheme which they hoped would frustrate the stand of the Church on plural marriage. They concocted a false revelation, allegedly given to President John Taylor in 1886, in which pretended secret authority was given to continue plural marriages.

On June 17, 1933, the First Presidency, under President Heber J. Grant, issued the following statement pertaining to this false revelation (italics have been added):

"It is alleged that on September 26, 1886, President John Taylor received a revelation from the Lord, the purported text of which is given in publications circulated apparently by or at the instance of this same organization.

"As to this pretended revelation it should be said that the archives of the Church contain no such revelation; the archives contain no record of any such revelation, *nor any evidence justifying a belief that any such revelation was ever given.*

"From the personal knowledge of some of us, from the uniform and common recollection of the presiding quorums of the Church, from the absence

in the Church archives of any evidence whatsoever
justifying any belief that such a revelation was given,
we are justified in affirming that *no such revelation
exists.*

"Furthermore, so far as the authorities of the
Church are concerned and so far as the members of
the Church are concerned, since this pretended revelation, if ever given, was never presented to and
adopted by the Church or by any council of the
Church, and since to the contrary, an inspired rule of
action, the Manifesto, was (subsequently to the pretended revelation) presented to and adopted by the
Church, which inspired rule in its terms, purport, and
effect was directly opposite to the interpretation given
to the pretended revelation, *the said pretended revelation could have no validity and no binding effect
and force upon Church members, and action under it
would be unauthorized, illegal, and void.*

"The second allegation made by the organization
and its members (as reported) is to the effect that
President John Taylor ordained and set apart several
men to perform marriage ceremonies (inferentially
polygamous or plural marriage ceremonies), and
gave to those so allegedly authorized the further
power to set others apart to do the same thing.

"*There is nothing in the records of the Church to
show that any such ordination or setting apart was
ever performed.* There is no recollection or report
among the officers of the Church to whom such an
incident would of necessity be known, that any such
action was ever taken.

"*Furthermore, any such action would have been
illegal and void because the Lord has laid down without qualification the principle that 'there is never
but one on the earth at a time on whom this power*

and the keys of this priesthood are conferred.' The Lord has never changed this rule.

"Moreover, four years after the date when it is alleged this pretended revelation was given to President John Taylor, and four years after the date of the alleged ordaining and setting apart of these men by President Taylor, to perform marriage ceremonies (presumably polygamous or plural), the Church in General Conference formally approved the solemn Declaration offered to the Conference by Lorenzo Snow, then President of the Council of the Twelve, that President Wilford Woodruff was 'the only man on the earth at the present time (1890) who holds the keys of the sealing ordinances.' *This statement would have been an unmitigated falsehood if the allegation of the organization were true. President Lorenzo Snow did not falsify.*

"Finally, without direct revelation from the Lord changing the principle that there is never but one man on the earth at one time who holds the keys of the sealing power — and we solemnly affirm that there is not now and there has not been given any revelation making any change in that principle — any such act of ordination by President Taylor as that seemingly alleged by the members of the organization would be completely null and void.

"No one better knew this principle regarding authority for this sealing power than President John Taylor and he would not have attempted to violate it.

"It is a sacrilege to his memory — the memory of a great and true Latter-day Saint, a prophet of the Lord — that these falsehoods should be broadcast by those who professed to be his friends while he lived.

"The Master said that in the last days, many should come in his name saying, 'I am Christ,' and that these would deceive many; that many false prophets would come who would deceive many; that false Christs and false prophets would arise, would show forth great signs and wonders, and would, if possible, deceive the very elect. The Lord warned us that in these days 'if any man shall say unto you, Lo here is Christ, or there; believe it not.'

"We do not wish to pass judgment upon or evaluate the motives of our fellow men — that is for the Lord to do — but we unqualifiedly say, as it is our right and duty to say, that the doctrines these persons preach and the practices they follow, *are born of the Evil One and are contrary to the revealed will and Word of the Lord.* We call upon them to repent and to forsake their false doctrines and evil practices. Unless they do so the Lord will not hold them guiltless.

"It is a significant fact that these claims are put forward in their detail after all persons who were in presiding authority at the time of these alleged occurrences and who might check the stories told, are dead.

"*Celestial marriage — that is, marriage for time and eternity — and polygamous or plural marriage are not synonymous terms. Monogamous marriages for time and eternity, solemnized in our temples in accordance with the word of the Lord and the laws of the Church, are Celestial marriages.*

"At President John Taylor's death, the keys of the sealing ordinances, with their powers and limitations, passed by regular devolution, in the way and manner prescribed by the Lord and in accordance with the custom of the Church, to President Wilford Woodruff.

"At the latter's death they similarly passed to President Lorenzo Snow; and upon his death, they similarly passed to President Joseph F. Smith; and at his death the same keys passed in the same way to President Heber J. Grant.

"There has been no change in the law of succession of the Priesthood and of the keys appertaining thereto, nor in the regular order of its descent.

"The keys of the sealing ordinance rest today solely in President Heber J. Grant, having so passed to him by the ordination prescribed by the Lord, at the hands of those having the authority to pass them, and whose authority has never been taken away by the Lord, nor suspended, nor interfered with by the Church.

"President Grant is the only man on the earth at this time who possesses these keys. He has never authorized any one to perform polygamous or plural marriages; he is not performing such marriages himself; he has not on his part violated nor is he violating the pledge he made to the Church, to the world, and to our government at the time of the Manifesto.

"Any one making statements contrary to the foregoing is innocently or maliciously telling that which is not true. Any one representing himself as authorized to perform such marriages is making a false representation.

"Any such ceremony performed by any person so making such representations is a false and mock ceremony.

"*Those living as husband and wife under and pursuant to the ceremonies proscribed by President*

PLURAL MARRIAGES WERE STOPPED BY NEW REVELATION WHICH SUPERSEDED PREVIOUS INSTRUCTION

April 6, 1904	Declaration of President Joseph F. Smith made effect of Manifesto worldwide.
January 8, 1900	Reaffirmation of the Manifesto by President Lorenzo Snow.
October 6, 1890	Manifesto issued by President Wilford Woodruff superseded the previous instruction allowing practice of plural marriage.
1886	Alleged Revelation (Fabrication)
July 12, 1843	Doctrine and Covenants 132

The Lord excused the Saints in Joseph Smith's day from building the temple at Far West because of their enemies. On the same basis he excused them in Wilford Woodruff's day from continuing to live the law of polygamy.

He did give Doctrine and Covenants 132 as a matter of restoring the principle. But then by revelation he also stopped it for a reason similar to that pertaining to the Far West Temple. The Manifesto put an end to all legal plural marriages. Even if the fabricated revelation allegedly given to President Taylor had been a fact, it too would have been cancelled by the later revelation of 1890 leading up to the Manifesto. The declaration of President Joseph F. Smith in 1904 made certain that the practice was stopped worldwide, not alone in the United States.

Smith or the ceremonies performed by any person whatsoever since that proscription, are living in adultery and are subject to the attaching penalties.

"We reaffirm as true today and as being true ever since it was made in 1904, the statement of President Smith which was endorsed by a General Conference of the Church 'that no such marriages have been solemnized with the sanction, consent, or knowledge of the Church of Jesus Christ of Latter-day Saints.'

"Finally, we are in honor bound to the government and people of the United States, upon a consideration we have fully received — Statehood — to discontinue the practice of polygamous or plural marriage, and Latter-day Saints will not violate their plighted faith.

"The Church reaffirms its adherence to the declarations of Wilford Woodruff, Lorenzo Snow and Joseph F. Smith.

"It adheres to the pledges made to the government of the United States, and to the Constitutional laws of the State of Utah.

"We confirm and renew the instructions given to Church officers by President Joseph F. Smith in 1904, in 1910, and in 1914, and direct the officers who administer the affairs of the Church diligently to investigate reported violations of the adopted rule, and if persons are found who have violated President Smith's ruling (adopted by the Church) or who are entering into or teaching, encouraging, or conspiring with others to enter into so-called polygamous or plural marriages, we instruct such officers to take action against such persons, and, finding them guilty, to excommunicate them from the Church in accord with the directions given by President Smith. We shall hold Church officers responsible for the proper performance of this duty.

"Heber J. Grant
"A. H. Ivins
"J. Reuben Clark, Jr.

"First Presidency"

Chapter 12

No Secret Ordinations

The Lord allows no secret instructions or ordinations in his church!

He has given none and will give none. As Paul told Agrippa, this work "was not done in a corner." (Acts 26:26.) It is in the open — it is public — it is for all to see and know.

Some cultists seek to confuse people by saying that the Lord has given secret revelations and secret ordinations authorizing "under the table" practices which for "public consumption" are supposed to be prohibited.

But the Lord is not two-faced. He does not deal in devious ways. What does he himself say about such claims of secrecy? He brands them as being false by requiring that all his acts be "known to the Church." Says he:

"Again, I say unto you, that it shall not be given to any one to go forth to preach my gospel, or to build up my church, except he be ordained by some one who has authority, and it is known to the church that he has authority and has been regularly ordained by the heads of the church." (D&C 42:11.)

He explained even further as he added: "He that is ordained of me shall come in at the gate and be ordained as I have told you before." (D&C 43:7.)

Then could any secret "ordination" be valid? He said even further: "All things shall be done by common consent in the church." (D&C 26:2.) And that means by public knowledge and public vote.

As the early elders complied with the law requiring licenses to preach, the Lord instructed: "The elders are to receive their licenses from other elders, by vote of the church" (D&C 20:63), and added:

"No person is to be ordained to any office in this church, where there is a regularly organized branch of the same, without the vote of that church." (D&C 20:65.)

And as pertaining to activities relating to the membership at large, as contrasted with strictly local or branch affairs, he said:

"And a commandment I give unto you, that you should fill all these offices and approve of those names which I have mentioned, or else disapprove of them *at my general conference*." (D&C 124:144. Italics added.)

Members of the Church should remember these basic principles, and remain alert to the Lord's law when cultists try to mislead them with teachings which are contrary to the scriptures.

Chapter 13

Only One Designated

There can be only one directing head in the Church of Jesus Christ on earth at any one time. God does not compete with himself.

Whenever a new president of the Church is chosen he must be called and installed in the precise manner set forth in scripture, for "no man taketh this honour unto himself, but he that is called of God, as was Aaron." (Heb. 5:4.)

But, in addition to his being made president of the Church, he also becomes the spokesman of the Lord to his people. The Lord allows for no contrary voice. He does not speak with a forked tongue, neither does he work against himself.

As the Church members by unanimous vote sustain a new president, they not only take upon themselves a great responsibility in pledging to follow him, but they also preserve a vital principle of the restored gospel of the Lord Jesus Christ. The vote is a covenant, made with uplifted hands before God and witnesses.

When we sustain a president, we agree to follow his direction. He is the mouthpiece of the Lord for today, and that has great and significant meaning. When this matter came up in the days of the Prophet Joseph Smith, the Lord speaking of his leaders said:

"They shall speak as they are moved upon by the Holy Ghost.

"And whatsoever they shall speak when moved upon by the Holy Ghost shall be scripture, shall be the will of the Lord, shall be the mind of the Lord, shall be the word of the Lord, shall be the voice of the Lord, and the power of God unto salvation." (D&C 68:3-4.)

As members of the Church, by voting to sustain our president, we place ourselves under a solemn covenant to give diligent heed to the words of eternal life as he gives them to us.

The modern word of the Lord says: "You shall live by every word that proceedeth forth from the mouth of God." (D&C 84:44.)

And how are we to receive that word? Through his properly appointed prophet!

That has been the divine pattern from the beginning. Through Amos (3:7) came the revelation saying:

"Surely the Lord God will do nothing, but he revealeth his secret unto his servants the prophets."

This was the Lord's pattern throughout the Old Testament. It was true in New Testament times. And it is true today.

When the modern Church was organized, the Lord made this clear by restoring the principle that the leader of his Church on earth shall also be his spokesman and not any self-appointed individual seeking to build up a following of his own.

On April 6, 1830, speaking of the newly appointed president of the Church, the Lord declared that his president shall also be his mouthpiece.

Having done so, the Lord designated him as prophet, seer and revelator.

And then the Lord commanded the membership as follows:

"Wherefore, meaning the church, thou shalt give heed unto all his words and commandments which he shall give unto you as he receiveth them, walking in all holiness before me;

"For his word ye shall receive, as if from mine own mouth, in all patience and faith." (D&C 21:4-5.)

Then followed this great promise if we will thus obey:

"For by doing these things the gates of hell shall not prevail against you; yea, and the Lord God will disperse the powers of darkness from before you, and cause the heavens to shake for your good, and his name's glory." (D&C 21:6.)

What more can we ask?

This points up a great principle — and an added lesson — that we must learn: There can be only one head of Christ's Church on earth at one time and he must be chosen and sustained in the particular manner set forth in scripture. No man can take it unto himself. He must be called of God as was Aaron. (Heb. 5.)

So we repeat: The Lord allows for no secret ordinations in his work. To be valid everything is done publicly and by the vote of the people.

This rules out cultists of all kinds, false teachers and false leaders of every description, and puts the Lord's people on notice that there is but one clear directing voice in the Church, and that is the voice of the prophet, seer and revelator, duly chosen by revelation and accepted by the vote of the people in the general conference of the Church.

President John Taylor, in speaking of the process of voting by which our president is sustained and which process we have constantly followed, said:

"This is the order that the Lord has instituted in Zion as it was in former times among Israel. . . . This is emphatically the voice of God and the voice of the people." (*Gospel Kingdom,* Bookcraft, p. 143.)

When President Brigham Young discussed this subject, he said:

"The Lord has but one mouth through which to make known his will to his people. When the Lord wishes to give a revelation to his people, when he wishes to reveal new items of doctrine to them, or administer chastisement, he will do it through the man whom he has appointed to that office and calling." (*Discourses of Brigham Young,* 1925 edition, p. 112.)

And that man is the president of the Church!

Brigham Young further said:

"The Almighty leads this Church and he will never suffer you to be led astray if you are found doing your duty." (*Discourses of Brigham Young,* p. 112.)

It was President Heber J. Grant who added:

"You have no need to fear that any man will ever stand at the head of the Church of Jesus Christ unless our Heavenly Father wants him there." (*Gospel Standards,* Deseret Book Co., p. 68.)

Now what authority does the president have?

As president of the Church, he holds all of the keys and powers given by the angels to the Prophet Joseph Smith in the restoration of the gospel in this last dispensation.

He receives these powers by the laying on of hands of those in authority.

I repeat — he receives all these powers by the laying on of hands of those already possessing them and holding the authority to give them to him.

Every president of the Church has possessed these keys and powers.

No president of the Church could function without them.

The Church itself could not function without them.

If the Prophet Joseph Smith had taken these keys of authority with him into the grave, could we do our work today?

We could not function without those keys. It is necessary that they be held in perpetuity by the leaders of the Church.

If Joseph had taken with him to the grave the keys of saving the dead, could we do our temple work?

Could we preach the gospel to every nation, kindred, tongue and people without the authority to do so?

If Joseph had taken with him into eternity the keys of the gathering of Israel, could Israel be gathered?

Would our pioneers have come to the tops of the mountains in fulfillment of the prophecies of both Isaiah and Micah and established here the headquarters of the Church unless they held the divine right to do so?

And there will yet be a worldwide gathering of the Lord's people before the second coming of the Savior.

Could this be done without the keys of gathering delivered to us by the prophet Moses, who held those keys and delivered them to Joseph Smith?

Could organized stakes of the Church be established in the far-flung areas of the world without the divine authority to do so?

We readily see, then, that the powers given by the angels to the Prophet Joseph Smith remained with the Church and they still remain with the Church. They are centered always in one man, the president of the Church, the prophet, seer and revelator.

It could not be any other way. This is the Lord's pattern. This is the way he directs and conducts his work.

Surely Amos spoke truly when he said:

". . . The Lord God will do nothing, but he revealeth his secret unto his servants the prophets." (Amos 3:7.)

In the words of President Wilford Woodruff:

"Let me exhort all elders of Israel and Saints of God to rise up in the majesty and dignity of their calling and make full proof of their ministry and covenant. Sustain by your works the authorities, keys and priesthood. The eyes of God, angels and men are over you, and when the work is finished, you will receive your just recompense." (Matthias F. Cowley, *Wilford Woodruff*, Bookcraft, p. 657.)

Chapter 14

The Church Is the Gate

When the Savior established his Church during his mortal ministry, and as it was further developed by the Twelve Apostles of that day, one important fact became conspicuously clear, which is:

That salvation comes through the Church.

It does not come through any separate organization or splinter group, nor to any private party as an individual. It comes only through the Church itself as the Lord established it.

It was the *Church* that was organized for the perfecting of the Saints.

It was the *Church* that was given for the work of the ministry.

It was the *Church* that was provided to edify the body of Christ, as Paul explained to the Ephesians. (Eph. 4:11-14.)

Therefore it is made clearly manifest that salvation is *in* the Church, and *of* the Church, and is obtained only *through* the Church.

The Lord established one strait and narrow way, and understandingly observed that "few there be that find it."

Not only did he provide that salvation should come through his regularly constituted Church, but he set up safeguards to protect its members from being tossed to and fro with every wind of doctrine and to preserve them from the sleight of men who, with cunning craftiness, lie in wait to deceive. (Eph. 4:14.)

Those safeguards, according to Paul's epistle to the Ephesians, rested primarily in the persons of the apostles and prophets whom God placed at the head of the Church for that specific purpose.

They were the inspired leaders. They were the spokesmen of the Lord, and their inspired messages to the people were the will of the Lord, the mind of the Lord, the voice of the Lord and the power of God unto salvation. (See D&C 68:4.)

With such heavenly guidance, need any go astray?

But there were men in the Lord's own day who taught false doctrines and led the people into mistaken paths. These the Savior severely criticized, accusing them of apostasy from the very law of Moses which they pretended to preach.

He said to them: "Did not Moses give you the law, and yet none of you keepeth the law?" (John 7:19.)

And again he said, "Had ye believed Moses, ye would have believed me: for he wrote of me." (John 5:46.)

What a sad commentary. Had the people believed Moses, instead of the crafty false teachers of their day, they would have accepted Christ, because Moses wrote of Christ. And if they had accepted Jesus, they would have received salvation through his Church.

But being blinded by false teachers, they rejected both Moses and Christ, and thus never joined the Lord's Church and hence did not receive the salvation which was available through it.

Obviously all of the writings of Moses are not in our Bibles of today, but in the Savior's time they must have been available, for Jesus criticized the elders and scribes for not believing what Moses said when he testified of Christ.

Isn't it interesting that Moses testified of the Savior, and that when the people would not believe Moses they therefore were not prepared to receive the Christ either? Do you recall that Paul said the law of Moses was a school-master to bring the people *to* Christ? (See Gal. 3:24-25.)

Not only did Moses write of the Lord, but the other prophets did likewise. Peter said, in speaking of Jesus: "To him give *all* the prophets witness, that through his name whosoever believeth in him shall receive remission of sins." (Acts 10:43. Italics added.)

We read in the twenty-eighth chapter of Acts that Paul, while he was in Rome, received many visitors "to whom he expounded and testified the kingdom of God, persuading them concerning Jesus, both out of the law of Moses and out of the prophets, from morning till evening." (Acts 28:23.)

Obviously therefore the scriptures available in that time spoke repeatedly of the Savior as all the prophets gave witness to him.

So there was no excuse for those who led the people astray, persuading them to crucify the Lord, knowing full well that the scripture spoke plainly of him.

The false teachers of New Testament times established cults of their own, separate and apart from the true work of God, and they, with their man-made traditions, formed the chief opposition to Jesus as he began his ministry.

You are familiar with the names of some of those cults. The Pharisees and the Sadducees are best known. Both were apostate in their teachings. Both were condemned by the Lord, and both developed the religious bigotry which eventually brought about the crucifixion.

An apostasy among the Savior's followers developed even during the Lord's own ministry. As early as the events recorded in the sixth chapter of John, this falling away took place. You will recall from reading that chapter in the New Testament that many of his disciples would not accept his pure doctrine and therefore fell away and no longer followed him.

In apparent dismay, Jesus turned to the Twelve and asked, "Will ye also go away?"

Then it was that Simon Peter replied, "Lord, to whom shall we go? thou hast the words of eternal life." (John 6:67-68.)

Note if you will that the words of eternal life were *not* with those who fell away, but rather with those who remained faithful and loyal.

Subsequently, during the administration of the Twelve, serious apostasy developed again. As a result, nearly all of the epistles of the New Testament were written to combat it.

Further evidence of early apostasy in the Church is brought forcefully and particularly to our attention by the manner in which Paul wrote his first letter to the Corinthians.

In it he testified that there can be no divisions in Christ. Rather, he said, "I beseech you, brethren, by the name of our Lord Jesus Christ, that ye all speak the same thing, and that there be no divisions among you; but that ye be perfectly joined together in the same mind and in the same judgment." (1 Cor. 1:10.)

Christ cannot be divided. There is no Savior but Jesus, and he saves only in his own strait and narrow way and not according to man-made creeds and rituals.

It is all-important then that members should not separate themselves from the true Church, nor apostatize from it, nor be guilty of behavior which would justify their excommunication.

If persons separate themselves from the Lord's Church, they thereby separate themselves from his means of salvation, for salvation is through the Church.

Some modern people have created cults of their own and among them are those who attempt to take refuge in section 85 of the Doctrine and Covenants.

They endeavor to say that the Church has gone astray, that the leaders are no longer inspired, and that "one mighty and strong" is needed to take over the affairs of the Lord. And without *any* evidence of modesty whatsoever on their parts, they themselves volunteer for the position.

There is one verse particularly in that section which they fail to consider. It is especially pertinent. It says that apostates and others who have been cut off from the Church will not be found among the Saints of the Most High at the last day. Why? Because salvation is in the Church, not elsewhere.

Listen to the Lord's words:

"And they who are of the High Priesthood, whose names are not found written in the book of the law, or that are found to have apostatized, or to have been cut off from the church, as well as the lesser priesthood, or the members, in that day shall not find an inheritance among the Saints of the Most High." (D&C 85:11.)

But cultists are not the only ones who are excommunicated from the Church. There are those who are cut off for moral transgressions and other infractions of the Lord's rules of behavior. They too should ponder this scripture most carefully.

If people believe in God at all, if they have any regard whatever for their own salvation, should they not realize, as is expressed in scripture, that salvation is through the Church, and that if people are cut off from the Church for any reason, they thus lose their inheritance in the kingdom of God?

President Brigham Young was very expressive in describing the fate of apostates when he said:

> "Why do people apostatize? You know, we are on the Old Ship Zion. We are in the midst of the ocean. A storm comes on, and as sailors say, she labors very hard.
>
> " 'I am not going to stay here,' says one. 'I don't believe this is the Ship Zion.'
>
> " 'But we are in the midst of the ocean,' says another.
>
> " 'I don't care, I am not going to stay here.'
>
> "Off goes his coat and he jumps overboard. Will he not be drowned? Yes. So with those who leave this Church. It *is* the Old Ship Zion. Let us stay on it."

And then he added:

> "If the candle of the Almighty does not shine from this place, you need not seek for its light anywhere else."

And then this mighty man in Israel declared:

> "Whenever there is a disposition manifested in any of the members of the Church to question the

right of the president of the whole Church to direct
in all things, you see manifested evidences of apostasy of a spirit which, if encouraged, will lead to a
separation from the Church and to final destruction.
Wherever there is a disposition to operate against any
legally appointed officer of this kingdom, no matter
in what capacity he is called to act, if persisted in,
it will be followed by the same results."

The language of the Lord is simple and easily understood. If any have apostatized from the Church or have
been cut off by the duly appointed courts provided by the
Lord, they shall not find an inheritance among the Saints
of the Most High unless they repent. (See D&C 85.)

Salvation is not to be found in splinter groups today
any more than it was to be found in the various denominations which polluted the teachings of Moses anciently or
which, in the days of early Christianity, transgressed the
laws, changed the ordinances and broke the everlasting
covenant.

The Lord says further in the same section of the Doctrine and Covenants:

"All they who are not found written in the book of
remembrance shall find none inheritance in that day,
but shall be cut asunder, and their portion shall be
appointed them among unbelievers, where are wailing
and gnashing of teeth." (85:9.)

There are some who claim that even though they are
excommunicated from the Church, their priesthood and
temple blessings are not taken away. Let us remind those
persons that the power to seal is also the power to loose,
for the Lord has said of his true servants, that "whatsoever thou shalt loose on earth shall be loosed in heaven."

(Matt. 16:19; D&C 132:46.) Excommunication takes away all rights, privileges and blessings of the Church.

What is so precious as salvation? And how is it to be obtained? Only through the Church and "being anxiously engaged" in its program.

There is no other way. If we are not valiant in the testimony of Jesus and if we fail to repent, we lose the crown over the kingdom and are assigned elsewhere. (D&C 76:79.)

But how wonderful is repentance. The Lord has said that if we will repent of our sins, and from then on keep all of his statutes, forgiveness will result and reformation is made possible.

What greater promise can the wayward expect?

The Lord came to save sinners. He taught that it is the sick who need the physician. Therefore, he invites the spiritually sick — as well as all others — to come unto him, repent, and be cleansed, sanctified, and saved in his kingdom.

"Have I any pleasure at all that the wicked should die? saith the Lord God: and not that he should return from his ways, and live?" (Ezek. 18:23.)

And so in his goodness and mercy, he calls out and says:

"Come unto me, all ye that labour and are heavy laden, and I will give you rest.

"Take my yoke upon you, and learn of me; for I am meek and lowly in heart: and ye shall find rest unto your souls.

"For my yoke is easy, and my burden is light." (Matt. 11:28-30.)

But let us remember that his yoke cannot be separated from his Church, and his burden requires that each one of us live by every word that proceedeth from the mouth of God. And the mouthpiece of God is the prophet, seer, revelator and president of his Church!

Chapter 15

One Mighty and Strong

Various of our apostates who become disenchanted
with the Church, and declare that its leaders have gone
astray, revert to section 85 of the Doctrine and Covenants
and read there concerning "one mighty and strong" destined
to set the Church in order.

They assume that this scripture refers to our day and
to our leaders whom they declare have fallen. But how
mistaken they are!

The leaders of the Church have not gone astray. They
are indeed and in fact the prophets, seers and revelators
of the Lord, even as were the brethren chosen when the
Church first saw the light of day.

Because there has been difficulty over that scripture for
years, the First Presidency, under President Joseph F.
Smith, published an explanation of it in the *Deseret News*,
November 13, 1905.

Their official statement in part is as follows and com-
prises the remainder of this chapter. (Italics have been
added.)

"The following has been issued by the Presidency
of the Church of Jesus Christ of Latter-day Saints

in explanation of verses 7 and 8 of Section 85 of the Doctrine and Covenants and is . . . authoritative:

"The following quotation is from the eighty-fifth section of the book of Doctrine and Covenants:

" 'And it shall come to pass that I, the Lord God, will send one mighty and strong, holding the scepter of power in his hand, clothed with light for a covering, whose mouth shall utter words, eternal words; while his bowels shall be a fountain of truth, to set in order the house of God, and to arrange by lot the inheritances of the saints whose names are found, and the names of their fathers, and of their children, enrolled in the book of the law of God;

" 'While that man, who was called of God and appointed, that putteth forth his hand to steady the ark of God, shall fall by the shaft of death, like as a tree that is smitten by the vivid shaft of lightning.'

"Perhaps no other passage in the revelations of the Lord in this dispensation has given rise to so much speculation as this one.

"Also it has been used by vain and foolish men to bolster up their vagaries of speculation and in some cases their pretensions to great power and high positions they were to attain in the Church. In a word, some have made claims that they were the particular individual mentioned in the revelation, the 'one mighty and strong, holding the scepter of power in his hand, clothed with light for a covering, whose mouth shall utter words, eternal words; while his bowels shall be a fountain of truth, to set in order the house of God, and to arrange by lot the inheritances of the Saints.'

"One would think in such a matter as this that sufficient native modesty would assert itself to restrain a man from announcing himself as the one upon whom such high honors are to be conferred, and who is to exercise such great powers in establishing the Saints in their inheritances; and that even if one suspected, for any reason, that such a position and such exceptional powers were to be conferred upon him, he would wait until the Lord would clearly indicate to the Church, as well as to himself, that he had been indeed sent of God to do the work of so noble a ministry, as is described in the passage under question.

"Those however, who have so far proclaimed themselves as being the 'one mighty and strong' have manifested the utmost ignorance of the things of God and the order of the Church.

"Indeed their insufferable ignorance and egotism have been at the bottom of all their pretensions, and the cause of all the trouble into which they have fallen.

"They seem not to have been aware of the fact that the Church of Christ and of the Saints is completely organized, and that when the man who shall be called upon to divide unto the Saints their inheritances comes, he will be designated by the inspiration of the Lord to the proper authorities of the Church, appointed and sustained according to the order provided for the government of the Church.

"So long as that Church remains in the earth — and we have the assurance from the Lord that it will now remain in the earth forever — the Saints need look for nothing of God's appointing that will be erratic, or irregular, or that smacks of starting over afresh, or that would ignore or overthrow the established order of things.

"The Saints should remember that they are living in the dispensation of the fulness of times, when the

Church of Christ is established in the earth for the last days and for the last time, and that God's Church is a Church of order, of law, and that there is no place for anarchy in it. (D&C 112:30; also sections 33:3; 43:28-31.). . . .

"As to the 'one mighty and strong,' some hold that he has come, others that he is yet to come. Some have held that the Prophet Joseph Smith was the man, and that he would be raised from the dead and appear among the Saints to fulfill the terms of this prophecy.

"Others have insisted that the late President Brigham Young was the man who fulfilled the prediction, when, with such heaven-inspired wisdom and masterly skill, he led the exiled Saints from Nauvoo to the Rocky Mountains and laid their settlements in the valleys of Utah.

"All these theories have been entertained and some of them by very good brethren; but good men, and even well-informed men, are sometimes mistaken, and all are capable of receiving larger information, and more and more light respecting the things which God reveals.

"The revelation from which the passage is quoted is a portion of a letter to William W. Phelps, written by the Prophet from Kirtland under date of November the 27th, 1832. William W. Phelps at the time was at Independence, Missouri. In order that the reader may have the whole matter before him, the letter is reproduced *in extenso* and the part afterwards accepted as the word of the Lord indicated:

" 'Kirtland, November 27, 1832

" 'Brother William W. Phelps — I say brother, because I feel so from the heart, and although it is not long since I wrote a letter unto you, yet I feel as though you would excuse me for writing this, as I have many things which I wish to communicate.

" 'Some things which I will mention in this letter, which are lying with great weight on my mind. I am well and my family also.

" 'God grant that you may enjoy the same, and yours, and all the brethren and sisters who remember to inquire after the commandments of the Lord, and the welfare of Zion, and such a being as myself; and while I dictate this letter, I fancy to myself that you are saying or thinking something similar to these words — "My God, great and mighty art thou, therefore show unto thy servant what shall become of all those who are essaying to come up unto Zion, in order to keep the commandments of God, and yet receive not their inheritance by consecrations, by order or deed from the bishop, the man that God has appointed in a legal way, agreeably to the law given to organize and regulate the Church, and all the affairs of the same."

" 'Brother William, in the love of God, having the most implicit confidence in you as a man of God, having obtained this confidence by a vision of heaven, therefore I will proceed to unfold to you some of the feelings of my heart, and to answer the question. [Here begins the revelation.]

" 'It is the duty of the Lord's clerk, whom he has appointed, to keep a history, and a general Church record of all things that transpire in Zion, and of all those who consecrate properties, and receive inheritances legally from the bishop; and also their manner of life, their faith, and works; and also of all the apostates who apostatize after receiving their inheritances.

" 'It is contrary to the will and commandment of God that those who receive not their inheritances by consecration, agreeably to his law, which he has given, that he may tithe his people, to prepare them against the day of vengeance and burning, should have their names enrolled with the people of God. Neither is their genealogy to be kept, or to be had where it may be found on any of the records or history of the Church. Their names shall not be found, neither the names of the fathers, nor the names of the children written in the book of the law of God, saith the Lord of Hosts.

" 'Yea, thus saith the still, small voice, which whispereth through and pierceth all things, and often times it maketh my bones to quake while it maketh manifest, saying: And it shall come to pass that I, the Lord God, will send one mighty and strong, holding the scepter of power in his hand, clothed with light for a covering, whose mouth shall utter words, eternal words; while his bowels shall be a fountain of truth, to set in order the house of God, and to arrange by lot the inheritances of the Saints whose names are found, and the names of their fathers, and of their children, enrolled in the book of the Law of God; while that man, who was called of God and appointed, that putteth forth his hand to steady the ark of God, shall fall by the shaft of death like as a tree that is smitten by the vivid shaft of lightning. And all they who are not found written in the Book of Remembrance shall find none inheritance in that day, but they shall be cut asunder, and their portion shall be appointed them among unbelievers, where are wailing and gnashing of teeth.

" 'These things I say not of myself; therefore, as the Lord speaketh, he will also fulfil. And they who are of the High Priesthood, whose names are not found written in the book of the law, or that are found to have apostatized, or to have been cut off from the Church, as well as the lesser priesthood, or the members, in that day shall not find an inheritance among the Saints of the Most High; therefore, it shall be done unto them, as unto the children of the priest, as will be found recorded in the second chapter and sixty-first and sixty-second verses of Ezra. [End of the revelation.]

" 'Now, Brother William, if what I have said is true, how careful men ought to be what they do in the last days, lest they are cut short of their expectations, and they that think they stand should fall, because they keep not the Lord's commandments, whilst you, who do the will of the Lord and keep his commandments, have need to rejoice with unspeakable joy, for such shall be exalted very high, and shall be lifted up in triumph above all the kingdoms of the world; but I must drop this subject at the beginning [of it].

" 'O Lord, when will the time come when Brother William, thy servant, and myself, shall behold the day that we may stand together and gaze upon eternal wisdom engraven upon the heavens, while the majesty of our God holdeth up the dark curtain until we may read the round of eternity, to the fullness and satisfaction of our immortal souls? O Lord God, deliver us in due time from the little narrow prison, almost, as it were, total darkness of paper, pen and ink — and a crooked, broken, scattered and imperfect language.

" 'I have obtained ten subscribers for the Star. Love for all the brethren.

" 'Yours in bonds, Amen.

" 'Joseph Smith, Jun.'

(*History of the Church,* Vol. II, 297-299.)

"It is to be observed first of all that the subject of this whole letter, as also the part of it subsequently accepted as a revelation, relates to the affairs of the Church in Missouri, the gathering of the Saints to that land and obtaining their inheritances under the law of consecration and stewardship; and the Prophet deals especially with the matter of what is to become of those who fail to receive their inheritances by order or deed from the bishop. The petition which the Prophet puts into the mouth of his correspondent, Elder Phelps, is:

" 'Show unto thy servant what shall become of all those who are essaying to come up unto Zion, in order to keep the commandments of God, and yet receive not their inheritance by consecrations, by order or deed from the bishop, the man that God has appointed in a legal way, agreeably to the law given to organize and regulate the Church, and all the affairs of the same.'

"This paragraph clearly proves that the subject in hand is the settling of the Saints in Missouri, granting them their inheritances, and the order of it all. In addition, the 'bishop,' who was Edward Partridge, is especially referred to as 'the man that God has appointed in a legal way, agreeably to the law given to organize and regulate the Church, and all the affairs of the same.'

"In the revelations by which Edward Partridge was called and appointed to stand as a bishop in the land of Zion — Missouri — the following occurs:

" 'And let my servant Edward Partridge stand in the office to which I have appointed him, and divide unto the Saints their inheritance, even as I have commanded; and also those whom he has appointed to assist him. . . . Let the bishop and the agent make preparations for those families which have been commanded to come to this land, as soon as possible, and plant them in their inheritance.' (D&C 57:7, 15.)

" 'For this cause [i.e., that the Saints might be gathered upon the land of Zion] I have sent you hither, and have selected my servant Edward Partridge, and have appointed unto him his mission in this land [i.e., Jackson County, Missouri].

" 'And whoso standeth in his mission is appointed to be a judge in Israel, like as it was in ancient days, to divide the lands of the heritage of God unto his children.' (D&C 58:14, 17.)

"This much, then, we have learned, viz., that Edward Partridge, the bishop of the Church, was the one 'called and appointed, to divide by lot unto the Saints their inheritances.' But was Edward Partridge the one in 1832 who was putting forth his hand to steady the ark and threatened with falling 'by the shaft of death, like as a tree that is smitten by the vivid shaft of lightning'? Undoubtedly.

"The brethren in those days were limited in their experience. The Church had been organized but as yesterday. The order of the priesthood was not understood then, as it is today. The brethren composing it had been but recently brought together. Some of them were often in rebellion against the Prophet and the order of the Church, because of these conditions; and it required instruction and time, and experience, to enable men to understand their duties and preserve their right relationship to each other as officers of the Church.

"Bishop Partridge was one of the brethren, who — though a most worthy man, one whom the Lord loved, and whom the Prophet described as 'a pattern of piety,' and 'one of the Lord's great men' — at times arrayed himself in opposition to the Prophet in those early days, and sought to correct him in his administration of the affairs of the Church; in other words, 'put forth his hand to steady the ark.'

"On the occasion of the Prophet's first visit to Independence, Missouri — Edward Partridge accompanied him — in the meetings and conferences held upon the land of Zion.

"Bishop Partridge several times strenuously opposed the measures of the Prophet, and was sharply reproved by the latter for his unbelief and hardness of heart.

"Indeed the apostate Ezra Booth, who was present, made the scene between the bishop and the Prophet one of the items that justified to him his apostasy.

"He refers to the circumstance in a letter, addressed to Bishop Partridge, which has been several times published in anti-'Mormon' literature.

"The bishop, moreover, was reproved for his 'blindness of heart and unbelief,' and warned of the danger of falling from his high station in a revelation given in August, 1831, while both he and the Prophet were still in Missouri:

" 'Yea, for this cause I have sent you hither, and have selected my servant Edward Partridge, and have appointed unto him his mission in this land. But if he repent not of his sins, which are unbelief and blindness of heart, let him take heed lest he fall.' (D&C 58:14-15.)

"All the foregoing occurred during the first visit of the Prophet to Missouri.

"In the latter part of April, 1832, the Prophet again visited the center place of Zion — Independence, Missouri. There were still ill feelings existing among the brethren, especially between Elder Rigdon and Bishop Partridge; but those difficulties were adjusted and Bishop Partridge, in the conference that was held on the twenty-sixth of April, gave to the Prophet the right hand of fellowship in behalf of the Church in Missouri, and acknowledged him to be the President of the High Priesthood of the Church.

"But notwithstanding the adjustment of all difficulties on this occasion, we learn from the correspondence that passed between the brethren of Kirtland and Independence, respectively, that the old difficulties in all their bitterness broke out afresh.

"Referring to this subject, Elders Orson Hyde and Hyrum Smith, who had been appointed by a council of high priests at Kirtland to write a letter of reproof and warning to 'Bishop Partridge, his council and the inhabitants of Zion,' say:

" 'At the time Joseph, Sidney [Rigdon], and Newell [K. Whitney] left Zion all matters of hardness and misunderstanding were settled and buried (as they supposed), and you gave them the hand of fellowship; but afterwards, you brought up all these things again in a censorious spirit, accusing Brother Joseph in rather an indirect way of seeking after monarchical power and authority. . . . It might not be amiss for you to call to mind the circumstances of the Nephites and the children of Israel rising up against their prophets and accusing them of seeking after kingly power, and see what befell them, and take warning before it is too late.'

"In a letter written by the Prophet himself on the same occasion, written to accompany a revelation which he was sending to Zion, he refers in very pointed words to the ill feeling existing towards him by the brethren in Zion:

" 'Though our brethren in Zion indulge in feelings towards us, which are not according to the requirements of the new covenant, yet, we have the satisfaction of knowing that the Lord approved of us, and has accepted us. . . . Repent, repent, is the voice of God to Zion. . . . I say to you (and what I say to you I say to all), hear the warning voice of God, lest Zion fall, and the Lord swear in his wrath the inhabitants of Zion shall not enter into his rest.'

"Also in a revelation given on the 22nd and 23rd of September, 1832 — five months after the reconciliation at Independence — the following occurs:

" 'And your minds in times past have been darkened because of unbelief, and because you have treated lightly the things you have received — which vanity and unbelief have brought the whole Church under condemnation.

" 'And this condemnation resteth upon the children of Zion, even all. And they shall remain under this condemnation until they repent and remember the new covenant, even the Book of Mormon and the former commandments which I have given them, not only to say, but to do according to that which I have written, that they may bring forth fruit meet for their Father's kingdom; otherwise there remaineth a scourge and judgment to be poured out upon the children of Zion. . . .

" 'But, verily I say unto all those to whom the kingdom has been given — from you it must be preached unto them, that they shall repent of their former evil works, for they are to be upbraided for their evil hearts of unbelief, and your brethren in

Zion for their rebellion against you at the time I sent you.' (D&C 84:54-58, 76.)

"It was while these conditions of rebellion, jealousy, pride, unbelief and hardness of heart prevailed among the brethren in Zion — Jackson County, Missouri — in all of which Bishop Partridge participated, that the words of the revelation taken from the letter to William W. Phelps of November 27, 1832, were written.

"The 'man who was called and appointed of God' to 'divide unto the Saints their inheritance' — Edward Partridge — was at that time out of order, neglecting his own duty and putting 'forth his hand to steady the ark'; hence he was warned of the judgment of God impending and the prediction was made that another 'one mighty and strong,' would be sent of God to take his place, to have his bishopric — one having the spirit and power of that high office resting upon him, by which he would have power to 'set in order the house of God and arrange by lot the inheritance of the Saints'; in other words, one who would do the work that Bishop Edward Partridge had been appointed to do but had failed to accomplish.

" 'But,' it will be asked, 'does Bishop Partridge fulfill the terms of the prophecy that related to the man falling 'by the shaft of death like as a tree that is smitten by the vivid shaft of lightning'? That should not be said without some qualification; although Edward Partridge died eight years later, in the forty-seventh year of his age, a victim of the persecution he suffered in Missouri.

"Edward Partridge in common with most of the Saints in Missouri, as a result of the reproof and warnings of the Prophet and others, was brought to a partial repentance; still, as late as March, 1833, notwithstanding the partial repentance referred to, the Lord expressed himself as being 'not well pleased' with Bishop Partridge and others.

" 'Behold, I say unto you that your brethren in Zion begin to repent, and the angels rejoice over them. Nevertheless, I am not well pleased with the many things; and I am not well pleased with my servant William E. M'Lellin, neither with my servant Sidney Gilbert; and the bishop also [Edward Partridge], and others have many things to repent of. But verily I say unto you, that I, the Lord, will contend with Zion, and plead with her strong ones, and chasten her until she overcomes and is clean before me.' (D&C 90:34-36.)

"Because of the failure of the Saints in Zion to fully repent and keep the commandments of the Lord, the fury of their enemies burst upon them, and they were driven from their possessions into exile, and their homes were destroyed. We have given the Lord's explanation of the troubles that came upon the people; it is found in a revelation given under date of December 16, 1833:

" 'Verily I say unto you, concerning your brethren who have been afflicted, and persecuted, and cast out from the land of their inheritance, I, the Lord, have suffered the affliction to come upon them, wherewith they have been afflicted, in consequence of their transgressions; yet I will own them, and they shall be mine in that day when I shall come to make up my jewels. Therefore, they must needs be chastened and tried, even as Abraham, who was commanded to offer up his only son. For all those who will not endure chastening, but deny me, cannot be sanctified.

Behold I say unto you, there were jarrings, and con-
tentions, and envyings, and strifes, and lustful and
covetous desires among them; therefore by these
things they polluted their inheritances.

" 'They were slow to hearken unto the voice of
the Lord their God; therefore, the Lord their God
is slow to hearken unto their prayers, to answer them
in the day of their trouble. In the day of their peace
they esteemed lightly my counsel; but, in the day of
their trouble, of necessity they feel after me. Verily
I say unto you, notwithstanding their sins, my bowels
are filled with compassion towards them. I will not
utterly cast them off, and in the day of wrath I will
remember mercy.' (D&C 101:1-9.)

"In the midst of the troublous times in Missouri,
Edward Partridge acted a most noble and self-
sacrificing part, and bore many indignities with the
greatest patience.

"He was taken to the public square at Independence, partly stripped of his clothing, and bedaubed
with tar and feathers amid the jeers of the mob.
He neither complained nor murmured at this treat-
ment, but bore it well, with meekness and dignity.

"He was one with five others who offered himself
as a ransom for the Church, 'willing to be scourged
or even put to death' if that would but satisfy the
tormentors of the Saints and stop the inhuman cruel-
ties practiced toward them by the Missourians.

"He was also active in settling the Saints in upper
Missouri in 1836-1838. He shared in all the labors
and hardships incident to the settlement of a new
country and subsequently passed through the trials

attendant upon the exodus of the Saints from Missouri.

"Who shall say that his repentance, his sacrifices, his sufferings and faithfulness, did not procure for him a mitigation of the severe judgment decreed against him in the revelation contained in the eighty-fifth section of the Doctrine and Covenants?

"At any rate, the Lord said, some three years later, that he was well pleased with Edward Partridge. The word of the Lord came to the Prophet to this effect on November 7, 1835:

" 'Behold I am well pleased with my servant Isaac Morley and my servant Edward Partridge because of the integrity of their hearts in laboring in my vineyard for the salvation of the souls of men. Verily I say unto you, their sins are forgiven them; therefore say unto them, in my name, that it is my will that they should tarry for a little season (in Kirtland) and attend the school and also the solemn assembly for a wise purpose in me. Even so, Amen.' (*History of the Church,* Vol. II, pages 302-303.)

"Certainly in the face of this plain statement of the Lord that the sins of Edward Partridge were forgiven him, we do not feel that his sad and early death was the fulfillment of the threatened judgment of the revelation. But *that he was the man so threatened in that revelation there can be no question;* not only on account of what is here set forth, but also because Orson Pratt, one familiar with Edward Partridge, and an active participant in all these historical matters, publicly declared from the pulpit in Salt Lake City, about the time of the death of President Young, that the man referred to in the passage of the revelation in question, was Bishop Edward Partridge.

"Of the fact of his statement there can be no doubt; and at the time he was historian of the Church as well as a member of the quorum of the apostles. . . .

"(Signed)

"Joseph F. Smith
"John R. Winder
"Anthon H. Lund

"First Presidency"

Chapter 16

Limiting Families

If we believe in God at all, we must likewise believe his commandments and keep them. If we expect to become perfect as God, then virtue must garnish our thoughts unceasingly. (D&C 121:45.)

The breakdown in morals during the past few years has been appalling in the extreme. It has not only been the promiscuity of youth, but it has been a breakdown of family integrity and fidelity, and it has included refusal of married couples to have children.

With it has come contraception, but even worse, abortion, which has gained such a hold in the western nations that in some areas there are as many abortions as there are live births.

In America the zero population growth pattern has about been reached. We now average even lower than the sought-for two children to the marriage.

This "family planning" is prominent in present philosophy. It is part of "the world," part of "the flesh," part of the conspiracy to flout the God of heaven whose advice is exactly opposite to these tactics.

Whom shall we serve? Whose word shall we take?

We are face to face with the wisdom of man versus the wisdom of God.

The Lord has given a specific commandment to married people: "Multiply and replenish the earth."

Advocates of family planning are now becoming "population control" advocates, too. They would use government compulsion to limit the number of children any family may have.

These individuals have inflicted a "scare program" upon the world, and upon the United States in particular, which has been referred to by some as the "nonsense explosion."

There is no more controversial subject today than the limitation of new births. Advocates say there are too many people and too few resources.

Scientists who have studied the energy and particularly the food conditions, and have done so seriously, dispute these extravagant claims.

They tell us that if our fuel resources are properly cared for, we will have sufficient for hundreds of years.

And when it comes to food, it is already demonstrated that proper farming is solving the food problems of such nations as India, Pakistan and Mexico. Better farming is the answer.

Experts tell us that the food shortage is not a problem of production altogether, but one of distribution, to a very large extent. But they also tell us that even in this vital matter, as people starve in some of the underprivileged nations, the black marketers are there, and that to a large extent in some areas these illegal operations are keeping the food from the hungry — food intended for free distribution — and forcing it into illicit sales.

More than gifts of food from other lands — gifts which too often end up on the black market — is needed by the underprivileged nations. They need *know-how*. They need technological instruction on how to be better farmers, how to raise more food more efficiently on their own farms. They need to be taught modern methods.

It is well known that where some of our American experts have taught farmers in other lands these better methods, production has been increased as much as fifteenfold over the original production per acre. Isn't that the answer?

One of the main difficulties about shipping food to these poorer nations is that when the grain does arrive, there are inadequate unloading facilities; once the grain is unloaded, there is no proper place to store it; and when it comes to distribution, there are very inadequate means of shipping.

The establishment of the free enterprise system is what these countries need. Under this system better farming could be taught, better loading docks could be built, storage places could be provided, and shipping facilities set up to assure fair distribution.

Think what such improvements would do to raise the entire standard of living. Could birth control pills do as well?

India, Pakistan, the Philippines and Mexico are already nearing self-sufficiency in grain production, with surpluses actually in view within the next thirty years, according to an Associated Press release quoting the Food and Agricultural Organization of the United Nations.

Stocks of butter and skim milk also have moved into the surplus class. Here is a portion of the recent FAO report:

"France has 151,000 tons of excess butter, a commodity particularly expensive and difficult to store because of deterioration. West Germany is saddled with excess butter stocks of 104,000 tons; the United Kingdom 750,000 tons; the United States 55,000 tons; New Zealand 52,000; Australia 24,000; Netherlands 40,000; Canada 15,000; Sweden 9,000; Belgium 7,000; Ireland 13,000; Finland 5,000; Switzerland 2,000 and the Soviet Union an unspecified surplus.

"The United States has 122,000 tons of surplus skim milk; Canada has 90,000 tons; France 60,000; West Germany 47,000; Belgium 30,000; Netherlands 22,000; the United Kingdom 13,000 and Switzerland 13,000 tons.

"In addition, Japan has a surplus of 5.6 million tons of rice and Brazil has surplus coffee in the amount of 2.6 million tons.

"None of the governments involved nor FAO has found a promising solution to the problem of too much food.

"If food is given away to the countries that need it, world trade would be affected adversely, FAO notes. Storage also presents problems. FAO estimates storage alone may cost 10 percent of the total value of grain per year. Butter costs even more to store because of spoilage."

When we consider world food surpluses, the arguments for birth control seem to lose their force. Reducing live births certainly will do the surplus dilemma no good, and it will have little effect on the starvation problem either. We need to get down to the basic reasons for distress among the underprivileged, instead of looking toward birth control as the panacea for all ills.

The Lord made it abundantly clear that when he created the earth, he did not set up any shortages. It is he who sends his spirits to the earth and he certainly provided sufficiently for them. Would we say that God is so short-sighted that he would not provide an earth which would support the number of spirits he plans to send here?

Did he not say: "The earth is full, and there is enough and to spare; yea, I have prepared all things"? (D&C 104:17.)

Why should Americans be afraid of overpopulation? Our farms are not up to full production. We have millions of idle acres not now used for farming which could be brought under cultivation. Washington, Oregon and Idaho farmers have provided an excellent example of what can be done. There they are opening up thousands of acres of new land, putting it under water through vast sprinkling systems, and are raising potatoes and grain to their hearts' content.

Look over America. Note its vast empty areas. Are we overpopulated?

New York City and Boston are crowded in their concentrated areas, of course; Los Angeles may have its full share of congestion, but what of Texas, Wyoming, Nevada, and Utah? What of the Dakotas and Minnesota? What of Oklahoma, Kansas and Arkansas, and many of the other states? Even look at most of New York State. Overpopulated? Hardly.

Then do American couples need to limit their families for fear of overpopulation here?

Are we so in danger of starving in America that we must no longer have children?

What if there are slums in great cities like New York, London, and Tokyo? It is obvious, of course, that those places are crowded, but this does not mean that the entire planet is running out of space. Although India has a major population problem with 570 million people crammed into a little more than a million square miles, it might be remembered that Australia has twice that much land and only one-fourth of the population of India. Canada, Brazil, and Russia all have vast empty spaces and although much of this space is jungle or steppe or desert, the Israelis in Palestine have demonstrated that technology and hard work can make even the most inhospitable land support new settlers.

Taken as a whole, the United States has only fifty-eight people per square mile, scarcely one-sixth of the density of Switzerland, and yet when visitors go to Switzerland they do not feel that country is overcrowded. About 70 percent of all Americans have jammed themselves together into about 2 percent of the land area. Half of the counties in the nation have lost population during the last decade. It is reliably estimated also that the world's farmers can feed a population forty times as large as that of today if proper agricultural methods were used.

Where would the world be today without the large families of the past?

It will be remembered that George Washington was one of ten children in his family. General Eisenhower, later President Eisenhower, was one of seven sons. Thomas Jefferson was third in a family of ten children. John F. Kennedy was one of nine. Thomas A. Edison was the last of seven children in his family and the father of Benjamin Franklin had seventeen children.

Think of our own Church for a moment. Joseph Smith, the Prophet, was the fifth of eleven children. Brigham Young was the ninth of eleven; John Taylor was the second of ten. Wilford Woodruff was the third of nine children. Lorenzo Snow was one of seven. The mother of Joseph F. Smith had eight children. Heber J. Grant was one of eight children of his father. George Albert Smith was the second of nineteen children of his father, and President David O. McKay was third of ten children.

It is acknowledged that there are many people in America who go to bed hungry every night, but it is not because this bulging nation is short of food. The difficulty is distribution; it is lack of employment planning; it is unnecessary high prices going to already wealthy operators. It is not overpopulation which is making some Americans hungry, it is human nature in the form of bad management and selfishness.

Then should our families bow to such conditions and accept them as reasons for birth control? Here we live in a land of plenty. Will we allow family planners to persuade us to disobey God and resist the advice of his holy prophets here on earth?

We are face to face with a decision: whose word shall we take, the advice of the family planners as they fire up the "nonsense explosion," or will we accept the word of God?

President Joseph F. Smith said this:

> "We say to our young people, get married, and marry aright. Marry in the faith, and let the ceremony be performed in the place God has appointed. Live so that you may be worthy of this blessing. . . .

> "The command which [God] gave in the beginning to multiply and replenish the earth is still in force upon the children of men. *Possibly no greater sin could be committed by the people who have embraced this gospel than to prevent or to destroy life. . . .*" (*Gospel Doctrine*, pp. 275, 276. Italics added.)

Choose whom you will serve — the family planners or the prophets of God.

Or to quote Joshua more explicitly: "If it seem evil unto you to serve the Lord, choose you this day whom ye will serve." (Josh. 24:15.)

What was it the wise man said? "Fear God, and keep his commandments, for this is the whole duty of man." (Eccles. 12:13.)

And how is it stated in modern revelation? "For you shall live by every word that proceedeth forth from the mouth of God. For the word of the Lord is truth, and whatsoever is truth is light, and whatsoever is light is Spirit, even the Spirit of Jesus Christ." (D&C 84:44.)

And what is the commandment of God to families? "Multiply and replenish the earth."

The First Presidency has been most explicit in regard to limitation of families.

They published the following statement in the *Deseret News* of January 27, 1973:

"In view of a recent decision of the United States Supreme Court, we feel it necessary to restate the position of the Church on abortion in order that there be no misunderstanding of our attitude.

"The Church opposes abortion and counsels its members not to submit to or perform an abortion except in the rare cases where, in the opinion of competent medical counsel, the life or good health of the mother is seriously endangered or where the pregnancy was caused by rape and produces serious emotional trauma in the mother. Even then it should be done only after counseling with the local presiding priesthood authority and after receiving divine confirmation through prayer.

"Abortion must be considered one of the most revolting and sinful practices in this day, when we are witnessing the frightening evidence of permissiveness leading to sexual immorality.

"Members of the Church guilty of being parties to the sin of abortion must be subjected to the disciplinary action of the councils of the Church as circumstances warrant. In dealing with this serious matter, it would be well to keep in mind the word of the Lord stated in the 59th Section of the Doctrine and Covenants, verse 6, 'Thou shalt not steal; neither commit adultery, nor kill, nor do anything like unto it.'

As to the amenability of the sin of abortion to the laws of repentance and forgiveness, we quote the following statement made by President David O. McKay and his counselors, Stephen L Richards and J. Reuben Clark Jr., which continues to represent the attitude and position of the Church:

" 'As the matter stands today, no definite statement has been made by the Lord one way or another regarding the crime of abortion. So far as is known, He has not listed it alongside the crime of the unpardonable sin and shedding of innocent human blood. That He has not done so would suggest that it is not in that class of crime and therefore that it will be amenable to the laws of repentance and forgiveness.'

"This quoted statement, however, should not, in any sense, be construed to minimize the seriousness of this revolting sin.

"Signed, The First Presidency."

Chapter 17

Other Leaders Speak

Family limitation is not new. It has been advocated for years, and even as much as a century ago our Church leaders warned the people against it.

Note just a few of their statements:

Brigham Young:

"There are multitudes of pure and holy spirits waiting to take tabernacles. Now what is our duty? To prepare tabernacles for them: to take a course that will not tend to drive those spirits into the families of the wicked, where they will be trained in wickedness, debauchery, and every species of crime. It is the duty of every righteous man and woman to prepare tabernacles for all the spirits they can." (*Journal of Discourses,* 4:56.)

Brigham Young:

"To check the increase of our race has its advocates among the influential and powerful circles of society in our nation and in other nations. The same practice existed 45 years ago, and various devices were used by married persons to prevent the expenses and responsibilities of a family of children, which they must have incurred had they suffered nature's laws to rule preeminent. That which was practiced then in fear and against reproving conscience is now boldly trumpeted abroad as one of the best means of ameliorating the miseries and sorrows of humanity. The wife of the servant man is the mother of eight or ten healthy children, while the wife of the master is the mother of one or two poor, sickly children, devoid of vitality and constitution, and of daughters, unfit, in their turn, to be mothers, and the health and vitality which nature has denied them through the irregularities of their parents are not repaired in the least by their education." (*Journal of Discourses,* 12:120-121.)

Wilford Woodruff:

"Another word of the Lord to me is that, it is the duty of these young men here in the land of Zion to take the daughters of Zion to wife, and prepare tabernacles for the spirits of men, which are the children of our Father in heaven. They are waiting for tabernacles, they are ordained to come here, and they ought to be born in the land of Zion instead of Babylon." (*Journal of Discourses,* 18:129.)

Joseph F. Smith:

"While man was yet immortal, before sin had entered the world, our Heavenly Father Himself performed the first marriage. He united our first parents in the bonds of holy matrimony and commanded them to be fruitful and to multiply and replenish the earth. This command has never been changed, abrogated or annulled; but it has continued in force throughout all the generations of mankind." (*Juvenile Instructor,* Vol. 37, p. 400, July 1, 1902.)

Joseph F. Smith:

"I regret, I think it is a crying evil, that there should exist a sentiment or a feeling among any members of the Church to curtail the birth of their children. I think that is a crime wherever it occurs, where husband and wife are in possession of health and vigor and are free from impurities that would be entailed upon their posterity. I believe that where people undertake to curtail or prevent the birth of their children that they are going to reap disappointment by and by. I have no hesitancy in saying that I believe that this is one of the greatest crimes of the world today, this evil practice." (*Gospel Doctrine,* pp. 278-279.)

Heber J. Grant:

"Providing opportunity for the spirit children of our Father in Heaven to come to earth and work out their own salvation is one of our sacred privileges and obligations." (*Improvement Era,* 44:329.)

The First Presidency:

"The Church of Jesus Christ of Latter-day Saints has always stood for the highest and purest ideals in family life. Marriage is ordained of God, and the paramount purpose of this sacred principle is to bring into the world immortal spirits to be reared in health and nobility of character, to fill the measure of their mortal existence. Married couples who, by inheritance and proper living, have themselves been blessed with mental and physical vigor are recreant to their duty if they refuse to meet the natural and rightful responsibility of parenthood. Of course, in every ideal home the health of the mother, as well as the intelligence and health of the children, should receive careful consideration." (April 1944.)

Melvin J. Ballard:

"There is a passage in our scriptures which the Latter-day Saints accept as divine: 'This is the glory of God — to bring to pass the immortality and eternal life of man.' Likewise we could say that this is the glory of men and women — to bring to pass the mortality of sons and daughters of God, to give earth-life to the waiting children of our Father. . . . The greatest mission of woman is to give life, earth-life, through honorable marriage, to the waiting spirits, our Father's spirit children who anxiously desire to come to dwell here in this mortal state. All the honor and glory that can come to men or women by the development of their talents, the homage and the praise they may receive from an applauding world, worshipping at their shrine of genius, is but a dim thing whose luster shall fade in comparison to the high honor, the eternal glory, the ever-enduring happiness that shall come to the woman who fulfills the first great duty and mission that devolves upon her to become the mother of sons and daughters of God." (*Sermons and Missionary Services,* pp. 203-204.)

John A. Widtsoe:

"The future of the state and of the race depends upon the willingness of its citizens to beget and rear children without artificial interference. During the last centuries mankind has learned much. The comforts and blessings in every modest home surpass those of the emperors of old. Who shall inherit these gifts and the others in process of making? — Our children, of course, if we have any, and if they are numerous enough to claim consideration. It is a cruel fact, to which we must give heed, that those of less training, or perhaps inferior gifts, continue fruitful; while those most highly prepared to enjoy and advance our civilization have a decreasing birthrate. Many a college class of picked men and women half a century after graduation have fewer children than the original number of the class. It takes more than two children to keep the population from decreasing. The worldwide view is the same. The birth rate of the more advanced nations is failing rapidly; while that of the more backward peoples is large and increasing." (*Evidences and Reconciliations,* Bookcraft, 1943 edition, p. 250.)

J. Reuben Clark, Jr.:

". . .behind the great principle and commandment (to multiply and replenish the earth) lies the eternity of the marriage covenant, the creation of bodies to tabernacle spirits that our Heavenly Father created and to bring them to this earth, so that they might have mortal bodies, live according to the commandments of God, that they might in their next estate begin and go on through all the eternities in eternal progression." (*Conference Report,* April 1951, p. 78.)

J. Reuben Clark, Jr.:

"It seems to me that the besetting sin today is sensuality, sex perversion, sex indulgence. There is some belief, too much I fear, that sex desire is planted in us solely for the pleasures of full gratification; that the begetting of children is only an unfortunate incident. The direct opposite is the fact. Sex desire was planted in us in order to be sure that bodies would be begotten to house the spirits; the pleasures of gratification of the desire is an incident, not the primary purpose of the desire. Remembering that fact, many problems will disappear, particularly the one presented by those who seek full gratification without begetting children." (Special Priesthood Meeting, October Conference, 1949.)

Stephen L Richards:

"To warn of a great danger, I must speak of it more specifically. I do so most reverently. If it shall please the Lord to send to your home a goodly number of children, I hope, I pray, you will not deny them entrance. If you should, it would cause you infinite sorrow and remorse. One has said that he could wish his worst enemy no more hell than this, that in the life to come someone might approach him and say, 'I might have come down into the land of America and done good beyond computation, but if I came at all I had to come through your home and you were not man enough or woman enough to receive me. You broke down the frail footway on which I must cross and then you thought you had done a clever thing.' " (*Conference Report,* October 1941, p. 108.)

David O. McKay:

"Some young couples enter into marriage and procrastinate the bringing of children into their homes. They are running a great risk. Marriage is for the purpose of rearing a family, and youth is the time to do it. I admire these young mothers with four or five children around them now, still young, happy." (*Church News,* Feb. 27, 1952, p. 3.)

David O. McKay:

"Seeking the pleasures of conjugality without a willingness to assume the responsibilities of rearing a family is one of the onslaughts that now batter at the structure of the American home. Intelligence and mutual consideration should be ever-present factors in determining the coming of children to the household. When the husband and wife are healthy and free from inherited weaknesses and disease that might be transplanted with injury to their offspring, the use of contraceptives is to be condemned." (*Improvement Era,* 51:618, 1948.)

Hugh B. Brown:

". . . the Church has always advised against birth control and that is the only position the Church can take in view of our beliefs with respect to the eternity of the marriage covenant and the purpose of this divine relationship. There are, of course, circumstances under which people are justified in regulating the size of their families.

"Where the health of the mother is concerned, and where the welfare of other children would be adversely affected, parents sometimes, under the advice of their physicians, deem it wisdom to take precautionary measures.

"On the other hand, there is no joy that comes into the hearts and lives of men and women comparable to that which comes with the birth of a little child and with the responsibility of its training, protection, and education. The President feels that the final decision in all these matters must be left with the persons concerned. The Church cannot give a blanket or over-all answer to the question which would be applicable to all situations. Seeking divine guidance and searching your own souls is recommended, but in a long lifetime of counseling on these matters, the General Authorities of the Church are united in recommending generally against birth control.

"We have no cases where young couples have come to us later in their married life and expressed regret that they had children. Thousands have come deploring the fact that they foolishly forbade the little ones to come. Sometimes because of artificial measures early in marriage nature takes a hand and it becomes impossible for the couple to have children, though it may be the greatest desire of their lives." (January 23, 1962.)

Joseph Fielding Smith:

"When a man and a woman are married and they agree, or covenant, to limit their offspring to two or three, and practice devices to accomplish this purpose, they are guilty of iniquity which eventually must be punished. Unfortunately this evil doctrine is being taught as a virtue by many people who consider themselves cultured and highly educated. It has even crept in among members of the Church and has been advocated in some of the classes within the Church.

"It should be understood definitely that this kind of doctrine is not only not advocated by the authorities of the Church, but also is condemned by them as wickedness in the sight of the Lord." (*Doctrines of Salvation*, Bookcraft, Vol. II, p. 87.)

Chapter 18

Family Responsibility

Two of the great counselors in First Presidencies of the Church have been outspoken on the matter of family relationships, family planning and limitation of children.

The following is from President J. Reuben Clark, Jr., given in one of his outstanding general conference addresses:

"During this conference much has been said about a subject that has been running in my mind for several months, and notwithstanding that it has been discussed so much, I should like to add a few words during the time I shall address you, of my own feeling about it. I am referring to the home and the family relationship.

"The family, looked at broadly, is as nearly basic to the principles and plan of the restored gospel as any principle of which I know. We have a Heavenly Father and Mother, the eternal parents of the spirits of us who are here. And those spirits were created that they might come to this earth and receive mortal tabernacles, so that in the due time of the Lord we shall lay away the mortal tabernacle; then in due time we shall resume it and become the perfect soul, the body and the spirit reunited.

"The Lord has created, so he has told us, worlds without number, and I am sure for this same purpose.

"I repeat, that family relationship is fundamental, because without it we cannot reach out to the destiny which our Heavenly Father has provided for us. When Adam came, he was alone. And the Lord said, 'It is not good that the man should be alone.' He said to Adam, 'Multiply, and replenish the earth.' (Gen. 1:28.)

"Eve came, then the command was given that a man 'shall cleave unto his wife,' leaving father, and mother, 'and they twain shall be one flesh.' (Matt. 19:5.)

"That was reiterated by the Savior replying to the query of the taunting Pharisees. And out of that union came ourselves, our mortal tabernacles.

"In our day the Lord has revealed another element, and that is the sealing of man and wife for time and for all eternity, and out of that union they twain beget blood and flesh.

"And I would like you to reflect upon the fact that our children came to us with spirits that did not ask us to bring them, but with spirits, through some operation of which I am not aware, that are assigned to us; and they come to us as our guests.

"We are responsible for the mortal tabernacling of that spirit; and I should like each and every Latter-day Saint to get that fact into his heart, that the child which is his, or hers, comes at the invitation, virtually, of them who beget it, and then I would like you to reflect upon the responsibility which that brings home to each and every man and woman who is a parent.

"Yours is the responsibility to see that this tabernacled spirit loses no opportunity, through you, to prove his worthiness and righteousness in living through his second estate.

"Now the point that I wish particularly to emphasize is this — you parents cannot shift that responsibility to anyone else. It is yours; you cannot divest yourselves of it.

"You cannot give it to the state, and you ought not to give it to the state, for when the state takes over the direction, instruction, and rearing of its youth, then passes out, as the whole history of the world shows, the great principle of free agency, and not only that, but all the sacred principles of chastity and morality, with a host of other virtues which belong to a free society and are inherent in the governing principles of the kingdom of God.

"You cannot entrust your children, in the sense of having them take over your responsibility, to our schools. They cannot do your work. They may aid, and, sometimes, they may detract and defeat. I have referred before to pernicious doctrines which are appearing in our schools, not only political doctrines, which I would like you to note, but moral.

"The doctrine that the sex urge is like the urge for food and drink, is born of Satan, and the man or woman who teaches it, is Satan-inspired. Every effort you can make to prevent the spread of this doctrine, you should make.

"You cannot entrust your children to society. That will never do. Society is too tolerant of wrong, too ignorant of matters of right living, too easy to betray and debauch.

"And lastly, the Church cannot take over the responsibility which is yours to train your children. The Church can aid, and should be the greatest aid; and we are derelict if we do not, as Church members and as Church organizations, provide that assistance.

"But beyond the Church — the Sunday Schools, the Mutual Improvement Associations, the Primary, the Relief Society, and all the priesthood organizations — beyond that is the family, and it is our responsibility as parents to see to it that we fully perform our duties in this respect."

President Stephen L Richards had this to say at the same conference:

"Perhaps the most serious aspect of this attack of the foe being made on our homes is the arbitrary curtailment of the size of families. The proponents of this worldly doctrine grow bolder and bolder every year.

"They claim support from mathematical prognostications as to the increasing demands of populations, and the limited supply of the earth's sustenance. They claim improvement of the race by its limitation.

"They have been making these claims for many years, and they have won many adherents to their cause, especially among the so-called intelligentsia of the world.

"For the most part the world has been under the leadership of this birth-restricting intelligentsia for many years. And where are we? We have more physical comfort, more education perhaps. Do we have better government? Are we making more progress in developing the Christian virtues among men?

TOKYO HAS THE LEAST CRIME OF
ANY MAJOR CITY. WHY?

Japan does not tolerate crime. During the past ten years the crime rate in New York City increased 300 percent, in West Berlin 200 percent, in London 160 percent . . . but in Tokyo it declined 10 percent and Tokyo is one-third larger than New York City. Reasons given from research:

1. Children are home for dinner — family closeness and loyalty.

2. Schools set aside two hours for moral and ethical education, stressing respect for others.

3. Japan is an island — there is no place to run and hide.

4. Japanese are workers — too busy for mischief.

5. Law is enforced in Japan. Tokyo police are modern and well equipped.

6. In Tokyo there are 1200 neighborhood stations. They patrol on bicycles or on foot and are alert to the presence of any stranger.

7. Every Tokyo policeman must visit every home in his neighborhood at least twice a year. This brings respect for police.

In Tokyo every crime is reported and most are punished. In Chicago 7 percent of criminals are indicted and only 3 percent of those are punished.

(*Congressional Record,* April 11, 1974, p. H2991.)

Do we have more brotherhood, peace, and unselfishness?

"I doubt if there exists in all the world any place or institution comparable to a big family for the inculcation of the principle of unselfishness and mutual consideration, the high qualities of character so indispensable in the solution of the world's problems.

"I know there are bad big families and bad small families; but take it by and large, I would assume that there is a thousand percent better chance of a great leader in a good cause coming from a family of ten than from a family of one.

"We know that he has commanded the replenishment of the earth from the homes of his people, as President Clark said yesterday. The Lord pity those who subject themselves to his rebuke for denying entrance to the spirit children whom he would send into mortality, and the Lord pity those sophisticated couples who would pervert the sacred institution of marriage into an arrangement for social convenience and selfish personal gratification.

"Now, fathers and mothers of the Church, some will conclude after hearing these comments that I am without sympathy for the sacrifice mothers make, and for the hardships put upon fathers in rearing a family in these oppressive economic times. Those who so conclude are partly right and partly wrong.

"I don't have too much sympathy for a father, a Latter-day Saint father, who decides that a baby cannot come into the home until a ten or fifteen thousand dollar house has been built and furnished, and the money is in the bank to pay expenses, and who will let his wife go to work to bring about this so-called security. I don't have too much sympathy for Latter-day Saint couples who do not have faith that if they do God's will, he will bless them.

"I do have sympathy, however, for all parents in these days in the Herculean effort required to keep children in the paths of virtue and truth. I have sympathy for the endurance, the sleepless nights of excruciating anxiety of parents who don't know where their children are and what they are doing; and my heart bleeds for the innocent ones who are the victims of disgrace brought upon their families by the sins of the wayward.

"I am persuaded, my brethren and sisters, that there is no remedial measure which offers more promise in the alleviation of domestic distress as affecting husband and wife, and parents and children than the firm establishment of the sacred and religious character of family life, marriage in the Church and in the temple; and, as a necessary adjunct thereto, the reestablishment of the God-given principle of sacrifice in discharging parental and filial obligations."

Chapter 19

Eternal Family Life

Our first Article of Faith teaches that we believe in God the Eternal Father. In other words, we believe that he *is* our Eternal Father. We are his children, and we therefore belong to his family.

Since we are to become like him — "perfect as your Father which is in heaven is perfect" — family life is vital to us. For this reason we marry in the temple, for this reason we have children of our own and rear them in the faith, so that they may continue in our family circle in the eternities.

"Lo, children are an heritage of the Lord: and the fruit of the womb is his reward.

"As arrows are in the hand of a mighty man; so are the children of the youth.

"Happy is the man that hath his quiver full of them: they shall not be ashamed, but they shall speak with the enemies in the gate." (Ps. 127:3-5.)

Good family life on this earth is vital to our enjoyment of family life in the eternities. Hence the great stress placed upon children and families among the Latter-day Saints. This doctrine is one of the most important in the gospel.

We therefore must accept the inspiring principle that God is our Father, and that if we are to become like him, we must become parents ourselves.

When Paul was on Mars' Hill he came to the altar marked "To the Unknown God" (Acts 17:19-34), and took advantage of that great opportunity. He was a great salesman as well as a great preacher, and when he saw this altar marked to the unknown god, immediately he proceeded to explain to them the true God, who was unknown to them because they were worshiping idols.

The true God, not being known to them, required definition, and therefore he provided it. You recall that when he spoke to them he said, among other things, that "we are the offspring of God." That is the very basis of our whole religion. We are the offspring of Almighty God.

How can this be? We are dual beings. Actually every one of us is a spirit, and our spirit occupies a body of flesh and bone. The spirit is the real person. Our spirit resembles our body, or rather our body was "tailored" to fit our spirit. The spirit bears the image and likeness of God, and the body, if normal, is in the image and likeness of the spirit. And the spirit is the offspring of Almighty God.

Paul said also, "We have had fathers of our flesh which corrected us, and we gave them reverence: shall we not much rather be in subjection unto the Father of spirits, and live?" (Heb. 12:9.)

So we, as spirits, were begotten of God. We are not products of creation in the usually understood sense. We obtained our being by birth and not by "manufacture." As we have the blood of our earthly parents flowing through our veins, so we have divinity within us, because our eternal spirits have a divine parentage.

President Joseph Fielding Smith said:

"We believe in the divine origin of man. Our faith is founded on the fact that God is our Father and that we are his children. As members of his family, we dwelt with him before the foundations of this earth were laid and he ordained and established the plan of salvation, whereby we gained the privilege of advancing and progressing as we are endeavoring to do. The God we worship is a glorified Being in whom all power and perfection dwell, and he has created man in his own image and likeness with those characteristics and attributes which he himself possesses."

President Joseph F. Smith, on that same subject, said this:

"Where did we come from? We came from God. Our spirits existed before they came to this world. They were in the councils of the heavens before the foundations of the earth were laid. We were there. We sang together with the heavenly hosts for joy when the foundations of the earth were laid, and when the plan of our existence upon this earth and redemption were mapped out. We were there. We were interested, and we took a part in this great preparation. These spirits — that is, you and I, our brothers and sisters — have been coming to this earth to take upon them tabernacles from the morn of creation until now, and will continue until the winding-up scene, until the spirits who were destined to come to this world have come and accomplished their mission in the flesh."

President Brigham Young talked about the same thing, and he said:

"Our Father in Heaven begat all the spirits that
ever were or ever will be upon this earth. Then the
Lord, by his power and wisdom, organized the mortal
tabernacle of man. We were made first spiritual,
and afterward temporal."

President Joseph Fielding Smith in his book *The Restoration of All Things,* pages 250-251, says:

"How uplifting and comforting is the thought that
the Father of Jesus Christ is in very deed our Father,
that we are in very deed his offspring. It is the
teaching of the Church of Jesus Christ of Latter-day
Saints that we all lived in the world of spirits and in
the presence of our Father before we came to this
earth to be clothed in bodies of flesh and bones. He
is our Father."

And then President Smith quotes Paul as follows:

" 'The Spirit itself beareth witness with our spirit,
that we are the children of God:

" 'And if children, then heirs; heirs of God, and
joint-heirs with Christ.' " (Rom. 8:16-17.)

That is a very significant expression: heirs of God and
joint-heirs with Jesus Christ. In the oath and covenant of
the priesthood the same thing is expressed. If the holders
of the priesthood will honor their priesthood, "all that my
Father hath shall be given unto [them]." (D&C 84:38.)
We inherit these things from God, providing we are worthy,
and the reason we can inherit them is that we are his children. We have his divinity within us. That gives us the
right of inheritance, and therefore we are heirs of God
and joint-heirs with Christ.

President Smith goes on in his book:

"Latter-day Saints believe not only that we have a Father in heaven, but also a Mother there. Why not have a mother as well as a father? Is there any blasphemy in this teaching?"

Being a child of God gives us a great opportunity. It means that we can become like him and then live with him eternally if we will but follow his rules.

Was not this the meaning that Jesus had in mind when he said, "Be ye therefore perfect, even as your Father which is in heaven is perfect"? (Matt. 5:48.) That is our goal and our objective.

But there are many distractions. Always there have been distractions, all down through the years.

There has developed in recent years what almost amounts to a cult in certain fields. This is a cult which points the finger of scorn at believers and would seek to make us ashamed of our faith. It is one which would have us reject the doctrine of a special creation and accept the unproven but timeworn theory that all life evolved from lower forms, that worms and microbes were our ancestors, and not God.

It teaches that God is not our father, but that our first progenitors were microscopic forms which came into existence spontaneously, without cause, without reason, and without purpose.

According to this theory of primordial life, man at one time developed from an ancestor which, as one writer described him, was "a hairy, four-legged beast which had a tail and pointed ears and lived in trees."

Which requires more faith, to believe that God is our Father, or that some monkey-like ape gave us birth? And which would you rather have as your father, a creeping ape or Almighty God?

Our religion tells us that God is our Father. Some so-called intellectuals who point the finger at religion have become so domineering in their attitude toward those who do not believe their ghastly theories that they assume an attitude almost approaching tyranny. In some circles it has become persecution. So severe is it among some that one researcher, Dr. Thomas Dwight, was led to say:

"The tyranny in the matter of evolution is overwhelming to a degree of which no outsider has any idea. How very few leaders in the field of science dare to tell the truth as to the state of their own minds. How many of them feel themselves forced in public to do lip service to a cult that they do not believe in."

But how glad we are for such men as Dr. Joseph W. Barker, former dean at Columbia University. In an address some time ago, given at Ripon University, he said that "some scientists have been misled by certain of their observations, and, as a result, came to conclusions which were atheistic." But now he says:

"Even the most pragmatic materialist in the face of present-day scientific knowledge is led to the inevitable conclusion that the heavens declare the glory of God and the firmament shows of his handiwork. As the children of Israel foreswore the worship of the golden calf and returned to that faith of Jehovah, so we have foresworn the crass mechanistic materialism and returned to that faith in God of which the psalmist of old sang, 'The earth is the Lord's . . . . and they that dwell therein.' " (Ps. 24:1.)

Our religion tells us that God is our Father, and that we lived with him before we were born on this earth. It tells us further that every creature, microscopic and otherwise, was made by him before it lived here on the earth, and also that each one was made as a spirit before it was made in the flesh here in mortality.

There were two creations, one in which God made all things in the spirit. That is, he made the real life, the real being, as a spirit, in the first creation. And then, in the second creation, he provided these mortal tabernacles in which he placed the spirits that he had created in the preexistence.

The Book of Moses is very specific on this subject:

"And now, behold, I say unto you, that these are the generations of the heaven and of the earth, when they were created, in the day that I, the Lord God, made the heaven and the earth;

"And every plant of the field before it was in the earth, and every herb of the field before it grew. For I, the Lord God, created all things, of which I have spoken, spiritually, before they were naturally upon the face of the earth. . . . in heaven created I them; and there was not yet flesh upon the earth, neither in the water, neither in the air." (Moses 3:4-5.)

These are significant words. God made all life in heaven, as spirits, which were the real persons — or the real creatures, as the case may be. Afterward he created the mortal part of life. But at the time he made the spirits there was no flesh "upon the earth, neither in the water, neither in the air." (Moses 3:5.)

There is another very interesting thing in the second chapter of Moses. He says that when God did place life here on the earth, he placed within each form the seed of reproduction with the power to reproduce after its own kind. He gave human beings the power to reproduce. We have within ourselves the seed to reproduce, but what do we reproduce? We reproduce after our own kind, don't we? The only reproduction among human beings is more human beings.

The Lord put seed in animals, likewise, so that animals can reproduce only after their own kind. The same is true in vegetable life. An apple will only bring forth an apple, and it will not bring forth a cucumber. God placed in every one of his creations the seed within itself to reproduce after its own kind.

Of course it was a great discovery when the scientists learned about genes, which keep the species true. But who made the genes? It was this same God, our Eternal Father, who decreed in the first place that everything must reproduce only after its own kind.

Genesis sustains the Book of Moses in this, and says that every plant was made "before it was in the earth, and every herb of the field before it grew." (Gen. 2:5.) And Genesis is very specific in declaring that all life was to reproduce after its own kind.

The sectarian people have a hard time understanding the idea that man is made in the image of God and that God looks like a human being. But having made all these rules, he having created all things and now reproducing us after his own kind, how could we be other than in the exact image and likeness of God?

It had to be that way, because we are the offspring of God. And since we are his offspring, and since the law is that everything should reproduce after its own kind, and inasmuch as God would not break his own laws, he reproduced after his own kind and thus man is in the image and likeness of God.

It is very interesting to read in section 77 of the Doctrine and Covenants some further information on this same subject. The Prophet Joseph Smith had difficulty understanding the Book of Revelation, and asked the Lord for some explanations. In section 77, certain explanations are made that have to do with this very subject. We learn from this section that in heaven beasts and fowls and creeping things exist as spirits. The scripture then says ". . . that which is spiritual being in the likeness of that which is temporal; and that which is temporal in the likeness of that which is spiritual." (D&C 77:2.)

So you see, the body matches the spirit, and the spirit was made in the preexistence. Therefore, the body that is made here fits the spirit that was made in the preexistence.

Notice the next part of this section: ". . . the spirit of man in the likeness of his person, as also the spirit of the beast and every other creature which God has created." (D&C 77:2.)

So in heaven God created the spirits of all forms of life as they appear in mortality, the mortal form being in the likeness of the spirit, with mankind being God's own offspring, his literal children, having the full capability of becoming like him.

President Joseph F. Smith taught that our personal identity is both fixed and indestructible, "just as fixed and indestructible as the identity of God the Father and Jesus Christ the Son. They cannot be any other than themselves." (*Gospel Doctrine,* p. 25.)

But he also gave us a further glimpse into this great doctrine, saying that as our identity is fixed in the hereafter, so it was likewise fixed during the period prior to our birth into earth life.

Since we had our origin as children of God, our identity was fixed in the preexistence even as it is preserved in the hereafter. It never has changed and never will change in the future.

Said President Smith: "We did not spring from spawn. Our spirits existed from the beginning, have existed always, and will continue forever.

> *"We did not pass through the ordeals of embodiment in the lesser animals in order to reach the perfection to which we have attained in manhood and womanhood, in the image and likeness of God. God was and is our Father, and His children were begotten in the flesh of His own image and likeness, male and female."* (*Gospel Doctrine,* p. 25. Italics added.)

He then spoke of reincarnation, which was one of the false teachings circulated in his day, and says: "It is absolutely repugnant to the very soul of man to think that a civilized intelligent being might become a dog, a cow, a cat; that he might be transformed into another shape, another being. It is opposed . . . to the great truth of God that he cannot change and his children cannot change. . . . Their identity can never be changed, worlds without end. Remember that. God has revealed these principles and I know they are true."

Is it any less repugnant then, to suppose that we sprang from lower forms of life, than to think that we might be reincarnated into them after death? Our identity does not change from one eternity to the other, it was not changed prior to our birth, and will not be changed after our birth.

President Smith was a prophet of God. He spoke the words of God and taught that man was always man — the offspring of God — with the possibility sometime of becoming "perfect, even as your Father which is in heaven is perfect." (Matt. 5:48.)

Isn't it natural for children to become like their parents?

President Smith then concluded: "Our young people are diligent students. They reach out after truth and knowledge with commendable zeal, and in doing so they must necessarily adopt for temporary use, many theories of men. . . . It is when these theories are settled upon as basic truth that trouble appears, and the searcher then stands in grave danger of being led hopelessly from the right way." (*Gospel Doctrine,* p. 38.)

We believe in our Articles of Faith. One of them says, "We believe that men will be punished for their own sins, and not for Adam's transgression." Do you believe there was an Adam, described in the scripture as the first man? Do you believe there was such a thing as Adam's transgression, sometimes called the Fall?

Can you believe in Adam and in Darwinian evolution at the same time? Our religion teaches that there was no death in the world before the Fall. Darwinism says there was death before Adam — or before the first human being. This then becomes one of the great hurdles for LDS anthropologists.

According to our doctrine, the fall of Adam and the process of death are inseparable. Death and Adam are inseparable; death and the resurrection are inseparable; the fall of Adam and the atonement of Christ are inseparable; Adam and Christ are inseparable.

If there was no Adam, there was no fall. If there was no fall of Adam, there was no atonement by Christ. If there was no atonement by Christ, our religion is in vain, for if there was no Adam, there was no Christ either. If there is no Christ, where are we?

Are we ready to reject our inspired religion, our faith in God and Christ, to accept the questionable philosophy that may be thrust upon us by some unbelieving, even atheistic, professor of an unproved hypothesis? This is certainly a case in point where we must do as Joshua of old said, "Choose you this day whom ye will serve." (Josh. 24:15.)

A Utah newspaper ran this editorial:

"A midwestern newspaper, in its editorial columns, defined the origin of language and said that primitive man was able to communicate only through facial expressions and bodily movements. It claimed that the spoken language came much later and was part of man's evolution to his present state. This, of course, is in line with other false hypotheses being foisted upon an unwary public, many of whom are willing to believe that if we developed from lower forms of life, we also had to develop language from lower forms.

"They say we learned to speak as we also learned to stand erect or to think, hunt, and eventually cultivate the ground. But how foolish is this notion in the light of revelation.

"The first man, Adam, could speak eloquently. He could write. He could talk, not only with other men but with God, who was his teacher, who likewise gave him his language and his intelligence.

"The earliest men, according to the scriptures, kept books of remembrance, and they wrote the scriptures themselves, under inspiration from the Almighty. Has there ever been more beautiful language than is found in the scriptures? Has any writing been as uplifting and enduring?

"Language did not evolve from lowly origins. It was beautiful to begin with. It suffered from the same retrogression that centuries ago made cavemen out of intelligent beings and turned pure religion into

superstition, as early men apostatized from God."
(*Church News,* March 2, 1974.)

Could Adam and his children read and write? The
scripture explains:

"And then began these men to call upon the name
of the Lord, and the Lord blessed them;

"And a book of remembrance was kept, in the
which was recorded, in the language of Adam, for it
was given unto as many as called upon God to write
by the spirit of inspiration;

*"And by them their children were taught to read
and write, having a language which was pure and
undefiled."* (Moses 6:4-6. Italics added.)

The apostle Paul had to fight for the principle that
there was a resurrection, that there was an Adam, and
that there was a Christ who came forth from the grave
and atoned for Adam's sin.

Paul was one of the great witnesses of Christ anciently.
We have many witnesses for Christ today. The apostle Paul
bore this testimony as it is recorded in 1 Corinthians 15:

"Now if Christ be preached that he rose from the
dead, how say some among you that there is no
resurrection of the dead?

"But if there be no resurrection of the dead, then
is Christ not risen:

"And if Christ be not risen, then is our preaching
vain, and your faith is also vain.

"Yea, and we are found false witnesses of God;
because we have testified of God that he raised up
Christ: whom he raised not up, if so be that the
dead rise not.

"For if the dead rise not, then is not Christ raised:

"And if Christ be not raised, your faith is vain; ye are yet in your sins." (Verses 12-17.)

"Else what shall they do which are baptized for the dead, if the dead rise not at all? why are they then baptized for the dead?" (Verse 29.)

"But now is Christ risen from the dead, and become the firstfruits of them that slept.

"For since by man came death, by man came also the resurrection of the dead.

"For as in Adam all die, even so in Christ shall all be made alive." (Verses 20-22.)

And then Paul continues, speaking of the first man, Adam, and then of the resurrection:

". . . flesh and blood cannot inherit the kingdom of God; neither doth corruption inherit incorruption. . . .

"For this corruptible must put on incorruption, and this mortal must put on immortality. . . .

"Death is swallowed up in victory.

"O death, where is thy sting? O grave, where is thy victory? . . .

"But thanks be to God, which giveth us the victory through our Lord Jesus Christ.

"Therefore, my beloved brethren, be ye stedfast, unmoveable, always abounding in the work of the Lord." (1 Cor. 15:50, 53-55, 57-58.)

Let us realize this great fact, that God reproduced himself and gave us the opportunity of sometime becoming like him, and he provides the means, which is the gospel of Christ, to help us to become like him.

It was not an idle statement, quoted by President Lorenzo Snow, that "as man is, God once was, and as God is, man may become."

That is why Jesus commanded us to become perfect as our Father which is in heaven is perfect. For this reason we must follow his way of life, his plan of development, the only plan which will permit us to reach this goal.

That is why we must not be like the world, even though we live in the world. That is why the apostle Peter declared that we are a chosen generation, a royal priesthood, an holy nation, a peculiar people, that we might indeed become like God our Father.

Chapter 20

A Choice to Make

In Old Testament times, Joshua, the great general of ancient Israel, spoke to the people and said:

"Choose you this day whom ye will serve; . . . but as for me and my house, we will serve the Lord." (Josh. 24:15.)

In the spirit of free agency as expressed in that statement — meaning the right to choose for ourselves where our allegiance shall be — let us look again at our first Article of Faith.

It reads: "We believe in God, the Eternal Father, and in His Son, Jesus Christ, and in the Holy Ghost."

The moment we speak of God being our Father, we come directly to the matter of the origin of man. And when we speak of the origin of man, immediately we find ourselves in the midst of a conflict of philosophies just as varied and contradictory as may be found in any other field of thought.

But in this conflict — if we are to accept the very foundation of our religion — we must take a stand, even as did Joshua of old. We must decide in our own minds regardless of the theories of men that God really is our

Eternal Father, and that we truly are his offspring as the apostle Paul said. (Acts 17:28-29.)

In the days of Joshua there were many beliefs and philosophies extant, even as there are today. The heart of the conflict in that day, so far as religion was concerned, centered in whether there were many gods or one true and living God; whether the pagan deities dwelt in images made with men's hands or whether the God of Abraham, who denounced images, was a living reality.

The pagan deities were so real in the minds of their believers that in the days of Elijah many supposed that these false gods could even bring down fire from heaven to consume an altar.

So widespread was the acceptance of false gods that it was the popular thing to worship them. Even King Solomon was deceived and although he had been greatly blessed by the true God, he nevertheless built altars to the false ones.

Paganism was so popular and widespread that it was considered by many to be a thing of evil to reject the idols whom they could see, in favor of the God of Abraham whom they could not see. Worship of Jehovah was a thing disdained by them, looked down upon, even scorned. But was it really evil to worship him in spite of all this public opinion?

Joshua did not think so, even in the face of serious opposition from some of his own people who had been deceived. Where would they turn if they rejected Jehovah? Would they be willing to accept a god of wood or stone as a substitute?

Those vacillating people had seen the power of Jehovah in operation, but now they were being swayed by public opinion among their neighbors with whom idolatry was so popular.

Whom would Joshua's people serve? Would it be the celebrated although false deities of their contemporaries, or the unpopular and often scorned Jehovah? Or would they try to mix the two, paying homage both to the gods of men and the God of Israel, to save face with both?

This is what King Solomon tried to do, as you recall, worshiping the true God in the temple on one hand and setting up idols for pagan worship on the other. And you remember the curse that came upon him as a result.

Joshua's people wanted to be like other nations — they had no great desire to be a peculiar group, set apart from the world. They apparently loved worldliness and wanted more of it.

Joshua knew their thinking and so challenged them. Did they really prefer the popularity of the world? Or would they be content with the unpopular religion of the true God? In the face of extensive public opinion, he declared: "If it seem evil unto you to serve the Lord, choose you this day whom ye will serve."

We of today have a similar choice to make concerning this same God of Israel.

Do we really believe him to be our Eternal Father? It is basic to the religion of the Latter-day Saints to so accept him. We firmly believe with the apostle Paul that we are God's offspring!

But many do not so believe. It is popular today to accept another and a different view of the origin of the human race. Many so-called intellectuals particularly regard it as a thing of evil, or at least of weakness or of ignorance, to believe in the literal fatherhood of God. They brand such doctrine as something long outdated, childish or even as a myth.

Our young people in school are concerned about this problem, for it is becoming a challenge to their faith.

Shall we believe in the divine origin of man, or shall we accept the theory that life developed otherwise?

Of course it is popular in some circles to accept the deductions of certain learned men concerning how life began. But does that make our belief in the divine origin of man a thing of evil?

Amidst the conflicting philosophies of today, we as Latter-day Saints are blessed with the true knowledge of the existence of God. When the worldly wise say there is no God and that we had our origin elsewhere, we need listen to them only as Joseph Smith listened to certain teachers of his day. We need not be led astray by them any more than he was.

Prophets are now again on the earth.

The living God speaks to them and therefore the wisdom they extend to us is inspired and accurate and true.

The philosophies of men remain in the speculative field.

Prophets are safer to follow than philosophers!

Revelation often is at variance with the teachings of men, even of some of the great scholars. The wisdom of man cannot be placed in the same category with the wisdom of God.

Man is imperfect. So are his teachings.

But revelation is sure and certain and true. God's word shall not fail, neither will it ever lead us astray.

By revelation we testify that God is our Eternal Father and that he gave us life. We declare further that Jesus Christ is his Divine Son, and that Jesus likewise is the Good Shepherd, as he himself said, our Savior and our Redeemer.

Dare we turn our backs upon him?

There are those who claim that he never lived. Others admit that he was a historical person, but say he was only a transient preacher, a good man to be sure, even a learned man (although there is no record that he ever went to school), but merely a man.

Jesus was conscious of such criticism in his own day. His rejection by the populace was not easy for him, for he had earnestly tried to do good wherever he went, feeding the multitude, healing the sick, even raising some of the dead. But so many turned against him that he asked even his few remaining disciples, "Will ye also go away?" (John 6:67.)

Toward the last he sweat drops of blood in his anguish, as he suffered in their behalf.

But although rejected by the masses and accepted by only a few, he nevertheless was the Good Shepherd, the Son of God.

No adverse public opinion could change that. No rules or laws or philosophies or denunciations, no amount of persecution, could alter that great fact. He was the Good Shepherd, and he taught the literal fatherhood of God.

But he was led as a lamb to the slaughter — the Shepherd now a Lamb — the sacrificial paschal Lamb — and was crucified.

But whose was the ultimate victory?

Was it the crucifiers? Or was it Christ's?

With what pity we now look back upon the blind and stubborn souls who scourged him and denounced him, and nailed him to the cross!

Whose life did they really take? Was it their own eternal life?

Then what souls were saved? The Marys, the Marthas, the Peters, the Jameses, the Pauls, men like John and Barnabas and women like Dorcas.

We believe that the glory of God is intelligence. The Lord commands us to learn of "things both in heaven and in earth, and under the earth; things which have been, things which are, things which must shortly come to pass; things which are at home, things which are abroad, the wars and perplexities of nations, and the judgments which are on the land, and a knowledge also of countries and of kingdoms." (D&C 88:79.)

We do not hide our heads in the sand. Of course we want to know what the world knows, but we are not bound to accept as demonstrated fact those things which still are in the realm of speculation. Let us leave theories where they are — as theories — and accept only as fact that which is proven to be so. We are under no obligation to believe every hypothesis that is proposed and we have no reason to allow suppositions and conjectures to overthrow our faith.

Our leaders teach by revelation. There is no speculation in revelation from God. We are led by divinely chosen prophets who testify that God is our literal Father, our spiritual progenitor, the parent of our own individual, personal selves.

It was President Joseph F. Smith as we have seen who revealed that our identity never changes, from eternity to eternity. We are never transformed into any other form or species, nor have we ever been. We are ourselves forever — we always have been and always will be. President Smith vigorously denied that we were born of spawn, but declared that we are God's literal children.

Think of some of our great basic teachings, and ask yourself if you will exchange them for unproven theories no matter how popular they may be.

Think of your faith in Christ. Who is he? He is the Son of God! But if God has no powers of procreation, how could he have a Son? How could the Deity give parentage to Christ? It was Jesus himself who said that God is his Father and our Father as well. Do we believe what he said? Or shall we reject it for some scholastic theory?

Shall we exchange our faith in God as our progenitor and Heavenly Father for a belief in descent from some crawling, creeping, dust-biting reptile, or some prehistoric viviparous primate which could swing from tree to tree with the greatest of ease and even hang by its tail?

Let us dwell for a moment on immortality and the resurrection.

Do you believe in immortality? Could immortality evolve from an amoebic type of origin, from some supposed life that sprang from no life at all? Is it not true that nothing comes from nothing?

Do you hope for a resurrection? If we choose to believe in an amoebalike origin, by what power shall we be resurrected from the dead?

And if there is no resurrection, what happens to our hope of survival after death? What will happen to family survival if there is no survival at all? Why bother with temple marriage? Why live the law of chastity? Why pray? Why go to church? Why be honest?

If there is no immortality, what a waste this life must be — what a waste of such brains as Moses and Paul, Shakespeare, Einstein, Millikan, Pasteur and Compton, and of such leaders as George Washington, Abraham Lincoln, Winston Churchill and many others.

It was Dr. Arthur H. Compton, Nobel prize winner, who discussed the attainments of the great men of the world in terms of immortality, and then asked: "Having thus perfected man, what shall Nature do with him? Annihilate him? What infinite waste!

"I prefer," said Compton, "to believe he lives on after death, continuing in a larger sphere, in cooperation with his Maker, the work he has here begun."

It was this same great scientist who said that "our world is controlled by a Supreme Intelligence which directs its development according to some great plan." (*Freedom of Man,* Yale University, p. 92.)

Then is it really evil to believe in the Lord — our Father — our progenitor — our God? Never! Rather let us say with Joshua, "As for me and my house, we will serve the Lord."

We Latter-day Saints believe in God as our Eternal Father, and in his Son, Jesus Christ, and in the Holy Ghost. We testify that as divine Persons, they live and move and have their being — and that our prophets have seen them and talked with them.

Chapter 21

Sex Is Sacred

The Lord Jesus Christ has given us a way of life which will bring happiness to all who truly follow him in this life and joy everlasting in the world to come.

One of his greatest laws pertains to morals.

Humanity will rise or fall through its attitude toward the law of chastity. If the world will honor virtue, it can expect to receive God's blessings, but if it persists in the practice of sodomy, adultery, and other perversions, it can expect only destruction, for the wages of sin is death.

It is this awesome fact that should frighten at least the Christian world into a realization that we are being hurled into an abyss of moral degradation. The so-called sex revolution is destroying us.

The *Sacramento Union,* in an editorial, warned that the stench of moral decay has become intolerable. It called for a reestablishment of the divine code of chastity before everything is lost.

The *Chicago Tribune* reported that venereal infection is now the nation's leading communicable disease, which is another index to the extent of our moral breakdown. Three thousand new cases of this dreadful plague are contracted in America every day, more than half of them among teenagers.

As people change their standards of right and wrong, they begin to suppose that what was sin a generation ago is no longer so. They say now that standards are relative things which may be altered at will through usage and desire, and that old-fashioned goodness now has turned into priggishness.

Many actually seem to think that the popular trend is what determines right or wrong, and that moral values change with public sentiment.

A mother wrote to a medical doctor who conducts a newspaper column and asked whether she should provide her daughter with a supply of "the pill" as she left to attend a boarding school. In writing to the doctor, the mother said: "Personally I don't approve of sexual relations outside of marriage, but I wonder if I should be realistic and supply my daughter with birth control pills, just in case."

Can any mother in her right mind take such a position? Has the writer of this letter never taught her daughter the Lord's law of chastity? Why does she dread pregnancy but apparently have no great fear for her daughter's loss of virtue?

Was this girl never taught about her bodily functions in the sanctity of a good home?

All children need to be taught the facts of life, but where that teaching is to be given has become a source of great controversy. Should it be provided publicly or in the privacy of the home?

Is it wise to give it openly in such a way as to create a desire for corruption?

Is it to be merged with the so-called sex revolution that already has brought about the greatest moral decline in our age, with a plague of social disease in its wake? Or can it more properly be used to teach a nation chastity and sobriety?

Have you ever asked yourselves why this sudden urge to teach sex in a public way? Is someone afraid that the rising generation will not know how to reproduce itself, and that the race thereby may die out?

How is it that we ourselves were brought into existence? Our parents received none of this kind of teaching when they went to school.

Who is competent to give wholesome sex instruction to our children without creating lust in their minds?

We must say with all the emphasis at our command that the proper teaching of sex requires also the teaching of complete chastity, whether that instruction is given in the home, the school or the Church. To do otherwise is nothing less than suicidal. To ignore chastity in such instruction can transform it into a course in youthful sex experimentation.

The experience of some European countries clearly confirms the fact that public sex education increases promiscuity and as promiscuity is multiplied, venereal disease spreads like wildfire.

In all fairness to the children, we must teach them that the use of sex is to be confined completely and exclusively within the bonds of sacred marriage. No free sex is permitted by the Lord. In his law promiscuity is adulterous.

God made sex, but not for entertainment. It was provided for a divinely appointed act of creation in which we, to this extent, become co-creators with him.

When schools are prevented from teaching anything of a spiritual nature, they are thereby disqualified from teaching sex at all, for in its very nature, sex is spiritual and inseparably connected with the creative work of God.

We are not animals, to dwell only in a physical world.

We are the offspring of God, learning in this life to become like him.

He decreed that human beings never shall indulge in sex outside of holy matrimony which he himself instituted.

This is his definition of chastity. This is what he requires of every man and every woman.

That is why — on the fiery slopes of Mt. Sinai — he declared: "Thou shalt not commit adultery."

That is why, in his Sermon on the Mount, the Savior taught that anyone who even looks upon another with lust, has committed adultery in his heart.

Sex education belongs in the home where parents can teach chastity in a spiritual environment as they reveal the facts of life to their children. There in all plainness the youngsters can be taught that procreation is part of the creative work of God and that therefore the act of replenishing the earth must be kept on the high plane of personal purity which God provides, free from all forms of perversion.

Unskilled parents guided by the Holy Spirit can learn to teach their children properly. In fact, God commands it, and who are we to disobey? Why do some educators attempt to supersede the parents' teaching children how to fulfill their responsibility?

Medical men warn of the skyrocketing rise of venereal disease in our armed forces and it is certainly something to fear. But what of the innocent children born from illicit relationships?

No one knows exactly how many of these children are now living in Vietnam. The figure may run well beyond the fifty thousand mark. In Japan there are known to be more than twenty thousand mixed bloods fathered by U.S. servicemen.

Other thousands of such illegitimates are in Germany, Thailand, Korea, and Taiwan.

Nearly all have been abandoned by their fathers who sought momentary "thrills," as they supposed, by cohabiting with foreign women, not thinking that their own flesh and blood — born of these illicit unions — would become abandoned orphans, shunned by nearly all who see them.

These unfortunates roam the streets, unwanted, uncared for, begging for a living.

It is said that one in every ten American soldiers has fathered a child by an Asian woman.

Who has the right to beget illegitimate children?

Who has the right to take the virtue of an Asian or any other girl, or to lose his own?

Which American — at home or abroad — has the right to abandon his own flesh and blood and forget that his illegitimate child ever existed?

Can the God of heaven, who holds us all accountable for our sins, overlook this wickedness?

Of what good are national days of prayer if we do not support our prayers by our good works? Will God strengthen the arms of fighting men who desecrate his most holy laws? Will he prosper a nation which apparently condones these illicit practices and does little more toward prevention than to provide prophylactics for men who indulge?

Are these fathers so lacking in natural affection that they are willing to completely forget and ignore their own offspring in a foreign land?

We sing, almost tearfully at times, "God Bless America."

But we are almost constrained to ask, "How can he?"

The venereal disease rate in our war occupation areas is frightening in the extreme. We welcomed our boys home as conquering heroes, but some of them brought back a plague of V.D. which can destroy them as well as the happiness of the wives they left at home and to whom they have been so untrue.

V.D. is a killer. It also maims, causes heart trouble, insanity, and blindness. It destroys homes, spreads corruption to innocent wives and blights the lives of helpless children.

Some people justify their immorality by saying that restrictions against it are merely religious rules which have no meaning any longer because there really isn't any God.

Thoughtful people now recognize the existence of Deity more than ever before. Persons of genuine intellect, the true researchers, the great philosophers and the outstanding educators not only acknowledge him but they also worship him.

It is the selfish element in the world which no longer accepts Deity. And why? Because they do not want to be interrupted in their ingrown pursuits and are so involved in their personal desires, passions, appetites and lusts, that they have no room left for sacred things. Therefore, in their selfishness they reject or ignore God.

To the true realist, God is a significant Presence who guides the ultimate destiny of the world. But let us never forget that one of his most basic laws concerns morality.

That law is irrevocable and inescapable and applies to all, whether we believe in God or not. Everyone is subject to its penalties no matter how they may try to ignore them. The wages of sin is death — even to the unbeliever!

Immorality is next to murder in God's category of crime and always brings in its wake both destruction and remorse, even to college students who carry the pill with a mother's consent.

True civilization is built upon a foundation of morality and spirituality. It is just possible that a rejection of these basic factors may bring about its fall. It was so with Greece and Rome. It can happen to us unless we repent.

Every one of us would do well to remember that the "mills of the gods grind slowly, but they grind exceeding small."

No one can flout the divine law with impunity.

Every right-thinking person should be willing even to die if necessary in defense of virtue, whether that death be physical or social.

"Thou shalt not commit adultery" will forever stand as an immutable law to all human beings. This generation may rationalize itself into complete intoxication with sin and proclaim to high heaven that it is old-fashioned to be clean, but it will yet wake up to the stern reality that God does not change and that the moral laws are his and not man's to shift with every whim.

Adultery is still next to murder in the Lord's category of crime.

Homosexuality was made a capital crime in the Bible.

It was the Almighty who decreed that men and women must cover their nakedness by wearing proper clothing.

No amount of rationalizing can change God's law. No amount of fashion designing can turn immodesty into virtue and no amount of popularity can change sin into righteousness.

Once again we Latter-day Saints affirm the reality of the existence of Jesus Christ. Once again, as his humble servants, we define his law of personal purity, and solemnly declare that sex sin is an abomination in the sight of God.

No one on earth can ever cancel the divine command which says, "Thou shalt not commit adultery."

Chapter 22

No True Worship
Without Chastity

Jesus of Nazareth was rejected by his people. Sensing it keenly, he said one day:

> "O Jerusalem, Jerusalem, which killest the prophets, and stonest them that are sent unto thee; how often would I have gathered thy children together, as a hen doth gather her brood under her wings, and ye would not!
>
> "Behold, your house is left unto you desolate. . . ." (Luke 13:34-35.)

From the beginning of time it has been the tendency of mankind to drift away from the Lord and to love darkness rather than light.

It began when Satan came among the children of Adam and Eve and tempted them and destroyed their faith. The result was that "men began from that time forth to be carnal, sensual, and devilish." (Moses 5:13.)

This departure from the ways of the Lord was an apostasy, and since that time apostasy has existed among us almost continuously. While groping for the truth, men have made their own religions, established their own moral codes, and have justified themselves in following them.

It was so likewise in the days of the Savior. He fought against the man-made doctrines of his contemporaries, and said that to use them in worship was of no value for they could save no one. He vigorously denounced the sensual living so characteristic of that day.

It was not long before apostasy developed within the Christian group itself. It occurred in various ways: partly in doctrine and ritual, and much in the daily habits of the people.

The apostle Paul said that this apostasy was characterized by mankind becoming "lovers of their own selves, covetous, boasters, proud, blasphemers, disobedient to parents, unthankful, unholy, without natural affection, truce-breakers, false accusers, incontinent, fierce, despisers of those that are good, traitors, heady, highminded, lovers of pleasures more than lovers of God; having a form of godliness, but denying the power thereof. . . ." (2 Tim. 3:2-5.)

Usually when people speak of an apostasy from the truth they refer to changes in doctrines or a repudiation of certain beliefs. There has been an abundance of this. Such changes have resulted in the organization of hundreds of churches with different creeds, rituals and ordinances, many of them being highly contradictory.

But personal sin is as real an apostasy as any effort to change the law or break the everlasting covenant.

Consider Paul's words again: covetous, proud, blasphemers, false accusers, incontinent, without natural affection, lovers of pleasure more than lovers of God.

In other words, personal sin is as much an apostasy from Christ as an acceptance of false doctrine and man-made rituals.

But it is even worse when clergymen, pretending to represent the Christ, compound their apostasy by actually leading people into serious personal sin, at the same time asking them to practice creeds of their own invention which have no power to save.

An Atlantic edition of *Time* magazine reported in its religious section that "the 20th Century's sexual revolution directly challenges Christianity's basic doctrines against immorality." The magazine then goes on to say:

"Some progressive church thinkers now advocate a 'new morality' to take account of these facts of life. What they propose is an ethic based on love rather than law in which the ultimate criterion for right and wrong is not divine command, but the individual's perception of what is good for himself."

The article referred to nine hundred clergymen and students of religion gathered at Harvard University's divinity school to ponder this so-called new morality. Many among those clergymen expressed the thought that this new moral concept which fosters licentious free love is what they call a "healthy advance" which now will relieve them of the responsibility of living the strict moral teachings of Christ.

A minister, speaking at Goucher College, Baltimore, told a group of young students that "sex is fun — premarital sex is beautiful — we all ought to relax and stop feeling guilty about our sexual activities, thoughts and desires." He was thus quoted by the Associated Press. The newspapers published his picture with the article on his attempt to reverse the divine law.

Several states in America have eased up on laws regulating immoral behavior. Legislators are being asked to rule that adultery should no longer be considered a crime; that homosexuals and other deviates should be allowed to practice their depravities legally and without restriction and that the age of consent for a child to enter public prostitution should be lowered to sixteen years.

This is not only true in America. Similar conditions are found elsewhere, with some clergymen and high government officials alike condoning and in some cases encouraging licentious practices.

This is one of the great evidences of the apostasy of mankind from the teachings of Christ.

To reject or try to change the moral law of God is to reject God.

To leave the path of virtue as set forth by Christ is an apostasy from Christ.

If any segment of Christianity attempts to change the moral law of God it will attack one of the most basic precepts of heaven, and will thereby place itself in the role of anti-Christ.

Let us ask — Is God, who the scriptures say is the same yesterday, today and forever, now changing his mind?

Does Jesus no longer believe what he taught when he was on earth?

He said that anyone who looks upon a woman with lust in mind, commits adultery in his heart. Note that he says — if we merely look upon another with lust — it is immoral.

Then what does he say about the completion of that act?

Does he call it beautiful as does the above-mentioned preacher? Is the Savior now to retreat before the clerics who advocate free love?

Is he to admit that he was mistaken nineteen centuries ago and say that he was not as well informed as these modern clergymen? Will he now withdraw from his position and say that he was too strict for human nature and that he was not realistic?

Has Christ changed his mind?

Is he less understanding than the preacher in Baltimore?

Does he know less than this minister about the urges, the drives and the temptations of adolescent youth?

If Christ has not changed his mind, can the modern clerics change it for him?

Will he approve a reversal of his teachings?

Will he acknowledge the men who try to make the change? Will he recognize them as his ordained servants?

Will we accept the churches which they represent?

Will he call them his own?

Will he say that the primrose path is now the road to heaven or that it has become a modern version of the straight and narrow way?

Will he sanction the teaching of immorality to young boys and girls by men who claim to act in his holy name?

For any man to attempt to change the moral law is like trying to change the Deity himself.

It is to ask the Almighty to condone the petting, the necking, the wicked intimacies and perversions which go on in the back seats of automobiles, in motel and hotel rooms, and on park lawns and benches.

It is asking him to sanction the wicked abortions which frequently follow.

It is inviting him to smile indulgently and sweetly on misguided young people as they sow the seeds of death and hell.

Easy morality is no morality at all. And certainly where there is no morality there is no true Christianity either.

No one can make free love a doctrine and practice of the true Church of God, despite all that may be said by the nine hundred clergymen at Harvard Divinity School, or by any other group of ministers or priests speaking before schools and youth groups.

These reverend gentlemen should remember what their own Bibles say. Or do they no longer believe the scriptures?

And if not, can they truthfully claim to be Christians — or ministers of a Christian God?

Apostasy through immorality is at least as bad as returning to paganism.

God still stays: "Thou shalt not commit adultery."

Christ still says: "Whosoever looketh upon a woman to lust after her hath committed adultery with her already in his heart."

And Paul still says of those who deviate from the path of virtue into some of the great perversions, "They which commit such things are worthy of death." (Rom. 1:32.)

Let our so-called progressive Christians beware, lest like the ancient scribes and Pharisees they find that their house too has become desolate.

In this modern day, God has restored his pure gospel and his divine Church. Again he teaches the truth about himself and the way to come back into his presence.

Part of that restoration is a restatement of the moral law.

Again comes his precept commanding: "Be ye clean that bear the vessels of the Lord."

Again he appeals for virtue — complete, chaste, unblemished purity — on the part of his followers, for no unclean thing can come into his presence.

By modern revelation he tells us that sex sin is next to murder in the divine category of crime.

Virtue is as much a part of the restored gospel as baptism and the resurrection.

Chastity is as vital to us as the law and the prophets.

The work of God cannot abide in the midst of iniquity.

His people must not partake of the sins of Babylon or they will cease to be his people.

Although we are in the world we cannot indulge in its corruption.

We Latter-day Saints have a great modern message. We announce that God has appeared in our day. He has raised up modern prophets who speak for him even as did Moses.

He has established his Church again in this generation. He is rearing a new and modern people — a priestly nation — a people of virtue and purity.

We have hundreds of thousands of youth in this heaven-blessed Church, and they must be taught the restored truth.

But they must know that this truth includes virtue as well as worship, and that there can be no true worship without chastity.

Youth of Zion:

Believe with all your hearts in the restored gospel as given us through the Prophet Joseph Smith.

Believe that this restored gospel is the way of truth and joy.

Know that wickedness never was happiness, but that obedience and chastity lead to the abundant life.

Know that virtue is a vital part of the restored gospel and never can be separated from it.

Know and understand that no man or set of men, whether clergymen, educators, or government officials, can change divine law. They are neither greater nor more intelligent than the Almighty.

The Lord asks us to be as clean as he is, so that we may be fit to enter into his presence and become like him, for that is our destiny.

Chapter 23

We Believe in Honesty

One of our Articles of Faith includes these words: "We believe in being honest . . . ." (Article of Faith 13.)

This is one of the most important tenets of our religion, and for many people it is one of the most difficult to live. Honesty is as basic to true Christianity as baptism or the resurrection of the dead. It is the foundation of all character development. Just as no man can see the kingdom of heaven without baptism, as explained by the Savior, so no dishonest man, except he repents, can see the kingdom of heaven.

Our Christian civilization is built upon integrity. Without it our way of life would collapse. If we allow dishonesty to weave itself into the fabric of our lives, we invite moral suicide.

Dishonesty in the world is appalling. The cost of major crime is shocking in the extreme, but petty crime involving far more people is becoming a national disgrace. It is almost incredible that here in the United States, for example, shoplifting costs our stores nearly three billion dollars a year. Most shoplifters are women and children.

Other types of petty crime cost American businessmen an additional billion dollars annually.

One hotel in New York in one year lost 18,000 towels, 355 silver coffee pots, 15,000 fingerbowls, and 100 Bibles.

Seventy-five percent of all insurance claims are estimated to be dishonest, costing insurance companies 350 million dollars a year in overpayments. Cheating in school is admitted by hosts of students.

And yet, lest we think that dishonesty is completely engulfing us, we should recall that department stores, for example, when reporting on their charge accounts, say that the rate of default is less than 2 percent. In one year fewer than two thousand people out of 102 million taxpayers were indicted for income tax fraud. It is estimated by revenue officials that 95 percent of all income is reported to the government.

In a recent survey of teenagers, it was most heartening to note that these young people said they want to live honestly in what they call "this dishonest world."

We claim to be a Christian people. But to what extent have true Christian principles become a part of our lives?

Are our daily habits indicative of a genuine Christian conversion?

Is our personal conduct a reflection of Christlike virtues?

Can any professed Christian be a Christian indeed if he is not honest?

What is the gospel for — merely to talk about?

Or is it something to *live,* to incorporate in our daily conduct?

The Savior said it is to assist us to become perfect in all we do, as perfect as God.

Then is there any place for deceit in a true Christian life?

Is not dishonesty an apostasy from Christ to the extent of our misbehavior?

Can we have a living faith in Christ without doing his works?

To profess belief in him and yet refuse to live his laws seems to be a dishonest act in itself.

The Christian religion cannot be separated from the Christian life, and there can be no Christian life without honesty.

When the Savior told us to love our neighbors as ourselves, he spoke of honesty.

When he told us to do unto others as we would be done by, he again spoke of honesty.

When he told us to go the extra mile, to give our cloak as well as our coat, if need be, and even to turn the other cheek, he again spoke of honesty.

When he advised us to reconcile any differences we may have with others, he spoke of honesty.

When he vigorously denounced the hypocrites, he defended the principle of honesty.

When he described the Good Samaritan, he extolled not only an act of mercy, but a man who was being honest with himself in regard to his fellowman.

When he taught us to love the Lord our God with all our hearts, he asked us to be honest both with God and ourselves.

When he told us to avoid judging other people, he again spoke of honesty.

When he blessed the pure in heart, the merciful, the meek, and those who hunger and thirst after righteousness, he glorified honesty.

When he taught repentance as a principle of salvation, he commanded us to bring honesty into our lives.

When he permitted us to seek remission of our sins through baptism, he expected us to do so honestly.

When he taught the moral law, again he taught us to be honest with ourselves, with our fellowmen, and with God.

When he said that we cannot serve both God and mammon, he spoke of this same principle of honest living.

When he commanded us to become perfect even as our Father in heaven, he most certainly taught the strictest kind of honesty.

When he said, "Except your righteousness shall exceed the righteousness of the scribes and Pharisees, ye shall in no case enter into the kingdom of heaven," he spoke of honesty and integrity. (Matt. 5:20.)

When he advised his listeners, "Lay not up for yourselves treasures upon earth, where moth and rust doth corrupt," again he spoke of honesty. (Matt. 6:19.)

When he said, "If thine eye be evil, thy whole body shall be full of darkness," he spoke of dishonesty. (Matt. 6:23.)

When he taught us to seek first the kingdom of God and his righteousness, he referred to sincerity of purpose, which is honesty.

He asked at one time: "Why beholdest thou the mote that is in thy brother's eye, but considerest not the beam that is in thine own eye?" In doing so, he held up the principle of honesty. (Matt. 7:3.)

When he counseled, "Enter ye in at the strait gate," he expected us to walk in straight paths, and to honestly and sincerely avoid crooked ways. (Matt. 7:13.)

And when he said, "Every good tree bringeth forth good fruit; but a corrupt tree bringeth forth evil fruit," he referred to honesty and its ugly opposite. (Matt. 7:17.)

He warned against devious ways by saying: ". . . fear not them which kill the body, but are not able to kill the soul: but rather, fear him which is able to destroy both soul and body in hell." (Matt. 10:28.)

And yet, how gracious he was in his kindly invitation to help us to overcome our evil tendencies: "Come unto me, all ye that labour and are heavy laden, and I will give you rest. Take my yoke upon you, and learn of me; for I am meek and lowly in heart: and ye shall find rest to your souls." (Matt. 11:28-29.)

Dishonesty is directly related to selfishness, which is its origin and source. Selfishness is at the root of nearly all the disorders which afflict us, and man's inhumanity to man continues to make countless thousands mourn.

If all mankind were honest, we could have heaven here on earth. We would have no need for armies or navies, nor even a policeman in the smallest community, for there would be no crime, no invasion of other people's rights, no violence of one person against another.

There would be no grounds for divorce, nor would we have errant husbands or unfaithful wives. Conflict between children and parents would disappear, and juvenile delinquency would come to an end.

But in our society, is there anything more widespread than the tendency to lie and deceive?

It is the lie of the drug peddler that tempts a child to indulge, and the lie of the seducer that persuades a girl to surrender her virtue.

It is the lie of the shyster that traps his victim in a fraudulent deal.

It is the lie of the tax evader that puts him behind bars, and the lie of the student that turns him into a cheat at school.

It is the lie of the child — and too often also of the parent — that creates the generation gap.

It is the lie of the shoddy workman that hides a faulty repair.

It is living lie upon lie that makes a man a hypocrite.

It is the lie of a husband or wife that leads to infidelity, and that of the embezzler that makes him falsify his books.

It is the desire to lie and cheat which turns a mother into a shoplifter and the child who assists her into a potential criminal.

It is the lie on the lips of the neighborhood gossip that brings character assassination to many innocent victims.

It is the dishonest one who seeks to take advantage of or to humiliate or to deliberately injure a fellow human being.

It is dishonesty in a householder which persuades him to cheat a little newsboy out of his collections for delivering his newspapers, or induces him to avoid paying his doctor bills.

It is the lie of a clergyman teaching pre-marital sex as a type of trial marriage which persuades a girl to lose her virtue. She may be naive or obtuse in accepting his word, but what a price he will have to pay at the judgment bar of God for saying there is no sin in pre-marital sex when he knows full well that the Almighty has thundered from the heights of Mt. Sinai: "Thou shalt not commit adultery."

It is the lie of the hypocrite who berates his wife and belittles his children and is a beast in the home, that persuades him to assume a pious role on Sunday and sing in the choir and partake of the sacred emblems of the Lord's supper.

It is the lie of the infatuated girl that deceives her parents as she enters a life of sin with a boy who would only drag her down.

We Latter-day Saints believe in God and because we believe in him we also believe there is a devil.

But the devil himself is a liar — the father of lies, and those who choose to cheat and lie and deceive and misrepresent become his slaves.

Is it any wonder that the scripture says:

> "These six things doth the Lord hate: yea, seven are an abomination unto him:
>
> "A proud look, a lying tongue, and hands that shed innocent blood,
>
> "An heart that deviseth wicked imaginations, feet that be swift in running to mischief,
>
> "A false witness that speaketh lies, and he that soweth discord among brethren." (Prov. 6:16-19.)

In the following verses, the scripture ties this outburst to another heinous sin — which is never without its lies and deception — that of lustful sex, which God says will destroy the soul.

In modern revelation the Lord describes the hell of the world to come as he lists those who will suffer it, and he says:

> "These are they who are liars, and sorcerers, and adulterers, and whoremongers, and whosoever loves and makes a lie.
>
> "These are they who suffer the wrath of God on earth.

"These are they who suffer the vengeance of eternal fire.

"These are they who are cast down to hell and suffer the wrath of Almighty God. . . ." (D&C 76:103-106.)

Most of us claim to be Christians, bearing the name of Christ and worshiping in his holy name. But are we really Christians at heart? Is our worship truly acceptable to him? This we may determine by asking if we truly keep his commandments.

If not, are we worthy to bear his name?

One man asked: "If you had to prove in court that you are a Christian, what would you use as evidence?"

Christians must learn that there is nothing Christlike in deception.

There is no righteousness in hypocrisy.

There is nothing good about a lie.

We must recognize that if we are not honest we are not clean in the eyes of God, and that no unclean thing may enter his presence.

To resort to dishonest practices is to apostatize from the Christian way of life.

Apostasy from Christ becomes anti-Christ, and who among us can afford that?

To be anti-Christ is to be against him, to fight against him, even in silent disobedience.

To fight against Christ is to put God out of our lives, and that above all things invites self-destruction.

Chapter 24

Warning of the Past

Three great civilizations have occupied the Western Hemisphere. Two have passed into oblivion.

Those that disappeared died by virtual suicide. They brought about their own extinction as they defiled the land and defied their God by extensive crime, sexual deviation, and other loathesome sins of almost every kind.

Now our modern nations have succeeded them in the occupancy of this hemisphere. Much of the corruption which is common among us today resembles in striking detail the degradation that afflicted them.

In most of the Americas, for example, we have an advancing crime rate which is staggering to say the least, reaching an annual cost to the public of more than forty billion dollars in the United States alone.

Our moral collapse is appalling. Because of promiscuity, the dreaded social diseases have reached the epidemic stage. One health official said that actually they have surpassed epidemic proportions, and he called the condition a plague. These social diseases now affect more people than any communicable disease except the common cold.

In one of our best-known western cities health officials estimate that one in every ten persons between the ages of fourteen and twenty-five has a venereal disease. It is almost unbelievable.

The *International Herald Tribune* reported that easy abortion has now removed the stigma from immorality, making free sex even freer still.

Our inconsistency in the present situation is frightening.

While millions now accept promiscuity as a way of life and excuse adultery even though it wrecks marriages and breaks up homes, at the same time we make it illegal to offer a prayer in some of our public places.

While we teach sex in schools and publicly portray the vilest of filth on the movie screen, we virtually make a criminal of a schoolteacher who would bring a Bible into the classroom or who might ask the students to recite the Lord's Prayer. So far have we lost our sense of values!

Some Americans protest reference to the Almighty in the Pledge of Allegiance to the flag while others would eliminate "In God We Trust" from our coins.

Church attendance in most denominations is falling off at a rapid rate. Bible sales are down 25 percent, and some members of the clergy have lost their faith.

The Almighty provided that we should observe a sacred Sabbath each week. We have flouted this law to his face, and most of us have turned his holy day into one of pleasure or of "business as usual," and yet the Sabbath was given as a symbol of allegiance to our Creator.

How true it is that "we first endure, then pity, then embrace" the repeated and relentless incursions of iniquity.

Are we caught in a tidal wave of atheism and its accompanying corruption?

Are we any better than the civilizations which preceded us in America and which were swept away because of iniquity?

Those civilizations were taught a stern lesson pertaining to their occupancy of this hemisphere.

They were told that this is a land of special significance to the Almighty and that only those nations which serve God may remain here.

We of today must heed this warning if we ourselves are to survive.

We do not say that sin in other parts of the world is less reprehensible, or to be excused in the least degree, for sin is always sin regardless of the philosophies of men and no matter where it appears.

But in the Western Hemisphere a different situation exists. God has dedicated this land to the work of his Beloved Son, the Lord Jesus Christ, and he will not tolerate continued desecration of it.

In so reserving this land for his divine purpose, he decreed "that whoso should possess this land of promise, from that time henceforth *and forever,* should serve him, the true and only God, or they should be swept off when the fulness of his wrath should come upon them." (Eth. 2:8. Italics added.)

In plain, blunt words then we are told that whatever nations occupy this land must serve God or die!

The great men of modern America have given us similar warnings, peculiarly enough.

A generation ago, Roger Babson, at that time one of our leading economists, said: "Only religion can prevent democratic rule from developing into mob rule. A nation can prosper only as its citizens are religious, intelligent, capable of service and eager to render it." And then this great man said, and it is something to which we should give careful attention: "Every great panic we have ever had has been foreshadowed by a general decline in observance of religious principles." (*Fundamentals of Prosperity.*)

Abraham Lincoln told the people of his day that "America need fear no danger from without. . . . If danger ever threatens the United States, it will come from within. As a nation of free men, we must live through all time or die by suicide." (Ludwig, *Lincoln,* p. 65.)

Then the Great Emancipator added this:

"We have grown in numbers, wealth and power. . . . But we have forgotten God. . . . It behooves us then to humble ourselves before the offended Power, to confess our national sins, and to pray for clemency and forgiveness." (Proclamation, March 30, 1863.)

It was George Washington, our first president, who said:

"We ought to be persuaded that the propitious smiles of heaven can never be expected on a nation that disregards the eternal rules of order and right which heaven itself has ordained." (Inaugural address.)

One of the most stern of all warnings came from the great statesman Daniel Webster when he said:

"If we and our posterity reject religious instruction and authority, violate the rules of eternal justice, trifle with the injunctions of morality and recklessly destroy the political constitution which holds us together, no one can tell how sudden a catastrophe may overwhelm us, that shall bury all our glory in profound obscurity." (New York Historical Society, 1852.)

God has revealed that in the last days he would warn the people through the voice of tempests, earthquakes and seas heaving themselves beyond their bounds. Do we hear his voice now and recognize it?

When an estimated half-million people are stricken in one hurricane in Pakistan, when one hundred thousand are left homeless in a single quake in Chile, and these two disasters come within a few weeks of each other, can we ignore the warnings which they give?

When two devastating hurricanes wipe out entire communities in Mississippi within a few months of each other, when oft-repeated earthquakes strike Los Angeles with death and a half-billion-dollar devastation, do we hear in them the voice of God as a fair warning to the rest of us?

Can we relax and feel at ease because we take out insurance against earthquakes, fire, and storm damage?

Can an insurance policy prevent a hurricane or stay an earthquake?

Who can control such awesome forces?

Who is the God of nature?

Who stood in a storm-tossed boat with a group of frightened fishermen and rebuked the storm by simply saying, "Peace be still," and the wind abated and there came a great calm?

The extinct American civilizations now speak to us out of the dust of the ages giving warning against the same conditions which brought them down to oblivion.

Listen to what they say!

The ancient prophets who lived in America among those destroyed civilizations saw us of today through the eye of revelation. They referred to us as "gentiles" and one of these prophets said:

> "O ye Gentiles, how can ye stand before the power
> of God, except ye shall repent and turn from your
> evil ways?

"Know ye not that ye are in the hands of God? Know ye not that he hath all power, and at his great command the earth shall be rolled together as a scroll?

"Therefore, repent ye, and humble yourselves before him, lest he shall come out in justice against you." (Morm. 5:22-24.)

Another ancient American prophet, long since dead and now speaking to us out of the dust said:

"Behold, this is a land which is choice above all other lands; wherefore he that doth possess it shall serve God or shall be swept off; for it is the everlasting decree of God. And it is not until the fulness of iniquity among the children of the land, that they are swept off.

"And this cometh unto you, O ye Gentiles, that ye may know the decrees of God — that ye may repent, and not continue in your iniquities until the fulness come, that ye may not bring down the fulness of the wrath of God upon you as the inhabitants of the land have hitherto done." (Eth. 2:10-11.)

Another ancient prophet who lived here in America fifteen hundred years ago said:

"Behold, I speak unto you as if ye were present, and yet ye are not. But behold, Jesus Christ hath shown you unto me, and I know your doing.

"And I know that ye do walk in the pride of your hearts; and there are none save a few only who do not lift themselves up in the pride of their hearts, unto the wearing of very fine apparel, unto envying, and strifes, and malice, and persecutions, and all manner of iniquities. . . ." (Morm. 8:35-36.)

There are many people on this Western Hemisphere who have in their veins the blood of some of the tribes of Israel. To them this prophet said:

"Know ye that ye are of the house of Israel.

"Know ye that ye must come unto repentance, or ye cannot be saved.

"Know ye that ye must come to the knowledge of your fathers, and repent of all your sins and iniquities, and believe in Jesus Christ, that he is the Son of God." (Morm. 7:2-3, 5.)

And then we have this, also pertaining to us who live today, and coming from another ancient American prophet who speaks out of the dust to us today:

"These things doth the Spirit manifest unto me; therefore I write unto you all. And for this cause I write unto you, that ye may know that ye must all stand before the judgment seat of Christ, yea, every soul who belongs to the whole human family of Adam; and ye must stand to be judged of your works, whether they be good or evil;

"And also that ye may believe the gospel of Jesus Christ, which ye shall have among you. . . ." (Morm. 3:20-21.)

And finally, one of the greatest of all the prophets who lived in ancient America spoke this to us who live today:

"I exhort you to remember these things; for the time speedily cometh that ye shall know that I lie not, for ye shall see me at the bar of God; and the Lord God will say unto you: Did I not declare my words unto you, which were written by this man, like as one crying from the dead, yea, even as one speaking out of the dust?

"And God shall show unto you, that that which I have written is true.

"And again I would exhort you that ye would come unto Christ, and lay hold upon every good gift, and touch not the evil gift, nor the unclean thing." (Moro. 10:27, 29-30.)

If the modern nations of the Americas will repent and serve the Lord, great blessings will be theirs, for the prophet has said:

"This is a choice land, and whatsoever nation shall possess it shall be free from bondage, and from captivity, and from all other nations under heaven, if they will but serve the God of the land who is Jesus Christ." (Eth. 2:12.)

How long will the Almighty be patient as we ignore or defy him?

Shall we comfort ourselves by accepting the philosophy which says that there is no God, that the Bible is but a myth, and that the Book of Mormon is not true, and that therefore repentance is unnecessary?

We testify that God does live, that he is the eternal judge of all mankind, and that all of us must face the record of our own deeds on his judgment day.

Jesus Christ does live. He is the God of this land. It is his gospel, and only his gospel, which can save us from destruction.

God grant that we may awaken to our plight, and change our course while there is yet time.

God help us to know that:

"He that soweth to his flesh shall of the flesh reap corruption; but he that soweth to the Spirit shall of the Spirit reap life everlasting." (Gal. 6:8.)

Index